Identifying, Assessing, and Treating Autism at School

Stephen E. Brock   Shane R. Jimerson
Robin L. Hansen

Identifying, Assessing, and Treating Autism at School

Springer

Stephen E. Brock
Department of Special Education,
    Rehabilitation, and School Psychology
California State University Sacramento
Sacramento, CA 95819-6079
USA
brock@csus.edu

Robin L. Hansen
Department of Pediatrics
M.I.N.D. Institute
University of California, Davis
Sacramento, CA 95817
USA
rlhansen@ucdavis.edu

Shane R. Jimerson
Counseling, Clinical, and
    School Psychology
Child and Adolescent Development
University of California, Santa Barbara
Santa Barbara, CA 93106
USA
jimerson@education.ucsb.edu

Library of Congress Control Number: 2005935327

ISBN 13: 978-0387-29601-2   e-ISBN 0-387-29602-6

Printed on acid-free paper.

Printed in the United States of America.

9 8 7 6 5 4 3 2

springer.com

This book is dedicated to all educational professionals committed to enhancing the lives of children, and to our own children:

> *Dyana and David Brock*
> *Gavin O'Brien Jimerson*
> *Heather and Lindsay Ulrey*

Acknowledgments

As with any project of this magnitude, we feel it important to acknowledge the individuals who contributed to our efforts. First, Dr. Brock would like to thank Natacha Akshoomoff and Bobbie Kohrt for their helpful reviews of the first draft of this book, Christa Cummings for her research assistance, Michael Slone for sharing his thoughts on case finding and screening, and Lynn Tomson and Jeanne Witcombe for facilitating his professional development in the area of autism. Dr. Jimerson would like to acknowledge Mary Skokut for her helpful review of chapter drafts, Suzanne Babko and Daniel Openden for their feedback regarding recent literature, and Professor Robert Koegel for his thoughtful and supportive comments as well as the inspiring and informative scholarship he conducts with Lynn Koegel and many talented students at the UCSB Autism Center. Finally, Dr. Hansen would like to acknowledge the endless support of her husband, Gordon Ulrey, her colleagues at the M.I.N.D. Institute, and the children and families who made the M.I.N.D. Institute a reality.

Stephen E. Brock
Shane R. Jimerson
Robin L. Hansen

Contents

Acknowledgments   vii

1   Introduction and Overview 1

2   Causes 10

3   Prevalence and Associated Conditions 21

4   Case Finding and Screening 33

5   Diagnostic Assessment 54

6   Psycho-educational Assessment 74

7   Treatment 88

Appendix   Autism Resources 99

References   107

Index   121

1
Introduction and Overview

Recent epidemiological studies have documented a worldwide increase in the number of individuals identified with autism over the past decade (Tidmarsh & Volkmar, 2003). Whereas early research suggested classic autism to be relatively rare (4 to 6 per 10,000 or about 1 per 2,000; Lotter, 1967), more recent findings suggest that when viewed as a spectrum of disorders and including children at the milder end of the spectrum (i.e., Asperger's Disorder and Pervasive Developmental Disorder—Not Otherwise Specified), autism is much more prevalent than previously thought (60 per 10,000 or approximately 1 per 160; Chakrabarti & Fombonne, 2001; Fombonne, 1999; 2003a; 2003b). Although improved diagnostic practices and expanded classification systems account for a portion of this increase, some researchers now believe that yet to be identified environmental factors may have emerged in recent decades that place infants and children at increased risk for developing autism (Ozonoff & Rogers, 2003). Regardless of the cause (or more likely the causes) of this increased rate of autism spectrum disorders (autism or ASD), it is clear that today's school professionals are more likely to identify and be asked to serve students with autism than in years past.

For instance, the results of a recent electronic survey of school psychologists found 95 percent of the respondents reported an increase in the number of students being referred for assessment of autism (Kohrt, 2004). On average the respondents reported seeing 8 students with autism per year. Not surprisingly, the increased incidence of autism has resulted in an increased number of children with this disability being served in special education programs. Specifically, between 1994 and 2003 the number of students with autism, served under the *Individuals with Disabilities Education Act* (IDEA), increased more than 600 percent (from 22,664 in 1994 to 141,022 in 2003; US Department of Education, 2005). Given this new reality, it is essential that school professionals better understand autism and become better prepared to identify and serve these students. Facilitating attainment of such knowledge and readiness is the primary goal of this book.

Why School Professionals Should Read This Book

In addition to the increased frequency of these disorders, there are several other reasons why school professionals should increase their knowledge of autism. In this section, we review some of the issues that have generated an imperative for school psychologists and other educators to become better prepared to address autism.

Early identification and intervention are important determinants of the course of autism. An important reason for devoting increased attention to autism is the fact that early identification is not only feasible but is also an important determinant of its course (Baird, Cass, & Slonims, 2003; Goin & Myers, 2004). Research suggests that 75 to 88 percent of children with Autistic Disorder show signs of this condition in the first two years of life, with 31 to 55 percent displaying symptoms in their first year (Young & Brewer, 2002). These data combined with additional research suggesting relatively substantial cortical plasticity during early development and findings that intensive early intervention results in improved outcomes for children with autism (Ozonoff & Rogers, 2003; Rogers, 1998; Rogers, 2001) have led to a consensus that such early intensive intervention is essential (Mastergeorge, Rogers, Corbett, & Solomon, 2003). Thus, it is critical for school professionals, in particular those working in infant and preschool settings, to ensure that children with autism are identified as soon as possible.

Not all children with autism will be identified before children enter school. Although it should be expected that most of the more severe cases of autism will be identified before children reach school age, it must be acknowledged that many will "slip through the cracks" and go undiagnosed until after they enter kindergarten. Howlin and Asgharian (1999) reported data from a survey conducted in the United Kingdom that reveals the average age of diagnosis (at the time of their survey) for children with Autistic Disorder was about 5.5 years. In particular, it is not unusual for students with milder forms of autism (i.e., Asperger's Disorder) to go undiagnosed until after school entry. Among this group the average age of diagnosis was reported to be 11 years. Autism was rarely diagnosed under the age of 5 years (Howlin & Asgharian, 1999). Consistent with these data is the fact that the number of children with autism served under *IDEA* reaches its peak among children ages 6 to 11 years (US Department of Education, 2003). Thus, it is critical for all school professionals (not just those working in infant and preschool settings) to understand autism and be vigilant for early indicators of these disorders.

Most children with autism are identified by school resources. In a study by Yeargin-Allsopp and colleagues (2003) of the 1996 prevalence of autism in Atlanta, it was found that only 3 percent of children with autism were identified solely by non-school resources. All other children were identified by a combination of school and non-school resources (57 percent), or by school resources alone (40 percent). Thus, it might be argued that school professionals are expected to be involved in the identification process.

Full inclusion of children with autism in general education classrooms. Finally, it is important to acknowledge that current research and practice are moving toward the integration of special and general education (Koegel & Koegel, 1995). Students with disabilities are increasingly placed in full-inclusion settings. In addition, the results of recent studies suggesting that there are fewer children with autism who are also diagnosed mentally retarded further increases the likelihood that these students will be mainstreamed (Chakrabarti & Fombonne, 2001). Consequently, today's school professionals are more likely to encounter children with autism during their careers. It is essential that both special and general educators alike have up-to-date information regarding autism.

The Autism Spectrum Disorders

As currently conceptualized, the term "autism" includes several different (yet overlapping) disorders. This section reviews the evolution and current conceptualizations of the autism spectrum disorders.

Evolution of the term "autism." According to Rau (2003), the term "autism" appears to have first been used by Swiss psychiatrist Eugen Bleuler in 1911. Derived from the Greek *autos* (self) and *ismos* (condition), Bleuler used the term to describe the concept of "turning inward on one's self" and applied it to adults with schizophrenia. In 1943, Leo Kanner first used the term "infantile autism" to describe a group of children who were socially isolated, behaviorally inflexible, and who had impaired communication. Initially viewed as a consequence of poor parenting, it was not until the 1960s, and recognition of the fact that many of these children had epilepsy, that the disorder began to be viewed as having a neurological basis (Bryson, Rogers, & Fombonne, 2003).

In 1980, infantile autism was first included in the third edition of the *Diagnostic and Statistical Manual* (DSM), within the category of Pervasive Developmental Disorders [American Psychiatric Association (APA), 1980]. Also occurring at about this time was a growing awareness that Kanner's autism (also referred to a *classic autism*) is the most extreme form of a spectrum of autistic disorders (Bryson et al., 2004).

Autistic Disorder is the contemporary classification used since the revision of *DSM*'s third edition (APA, 1987). Currently, in the fourth edition of *DSM* (2000), Autistic Disorder is placed within the subclass of "Disorders Usually First Diagnosed in Infancy, Childhood, or Adolescence" known as "Pervasive Developmental Disorders." In addition to Autistic Disorder, the other specific Pervasive Developmental Disorders (PDD) include Asperger's Disorder, Pervasive Developmental Disorder, Not Otherwise Specified (PDD-NOS), Rett's Disorder, and Childhood Disintegrative Disorder. Figure 1.1 illustrates the relationships among these PDDs.

For the purposes of this book, the terms "autism" and "autism spectrum disorder" (ASD) are used to refer to a group of five specific diagnoses found within the

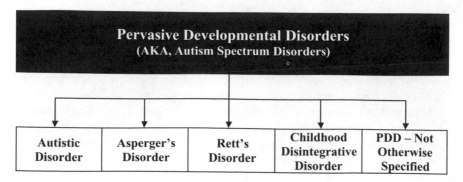

FIGURE 1.1. According to the *DSM IV-TR* (APA, 2000), Pervasive Developmental Disorders (or PDD) include five different diagnostic categories.

Diagnostic and Statistical Manual of Mental Disorders (*DSM IV-TR*; APA, 2000). The reason for this choice of terminology is that autism has been suggested to be much more readily recognized and understood by parents and professionals than PDD (Baird et al., 2003). Each of these five PDDs (or autism spectrum disorders) is briefly described below.

Autistic Disorder. This is the form of autism most like Kanner's infantile autism and is sometimes referred to as classic autism. The primary symptoms of Autistic Disorder are "markedly abnormal or impaired development in social interaction and communication and a markedly restricted repertoire of activity and interests" (APA, 2000, p. 70). Diagnosis requires the presence of 6 or more of 12 symptoms, with at least two being symptoms of impaired social interactions, at least one being a symptom of impaired communication, and at least one being a symptom of restricted repertoire of activities and interests. Tidmarsh and Volkmar (2003) offer the following description of what they consider a "typical example" of a child with Autistic Disorder:

... a 3-year-old child who does not speak and does not respond when parents call his or her name. Such children seem to be in their own world when left alone; in day care, they tend to isolate themselves from the group. They do not play with toys but, instead, perhaps repetitively stack blocks or push a toy car back and forth while lying on the floor. They are sensitive to loud noises and cover their ears when trucks pass by. They flap their hands and turn their bodies in circles. (p. 518)

Although they do have much in common, the manifestations of Autistic Disorder vary greatly across individuals, and many individuals diagnosed with autism do not display all of the characteristics (Travis & Sigman, 2000). As illustrated in Figure 1.2, Autistic Disorder symptom severity falls along a continuum. Among many children with autism, there is an associated diagnosis of mental retardation (Fombonne, 1999; Ghaziuddin, 2000; National Institute of Mental Health, 1997).

The long-term prognosis for individuals with autism also varies greatly, depending on the timing and effectiveness of interventions utilized and the degree of

Social Interaction

Socially Unaware	Limited Social Interaction	Tolerates Social Interactions	Interested in Social Interactions
Aloof	One-way interactions	Two-way interactions	Two-way & spontaneous
Indifferent	To meet own needs	Accepts approaches	One-sided
Interaction may be aversive	Treats others as tools & interchangeable	Replies if approached	Awkward
Solitary play	Prefers solitary play	Parallel play	Associative play

Communication

No Language System	Limited Language System	Idiosyncratic Language System	Grammatical Language System
Nonverbal	Mostly echolalic	Replies if approached	Spontaneous & two way
Noncommunicative	One-way	Incorrect pronoun & preposition usage	Tends to be one sided
	Used to meet needs	Odd constructions	Minimal, stereotyped, repetitive behavior

Restricted Repertoire of Behaviors, Activities, and Interests

Simple & Body Directed	Simple & Object Directed	Complex Routines, Manipulations, & Movements	Verbal Abstract Behavior/Interests
Internal	External	External	External
Very restricted range	Restricted range	Restricted ranged	Restricted range
Very marked, stereotyped, repetitive behavior	Marked, stereotyped, repetitive behavior	Occasional, repetitive behavior	Minimal, stereotyped, repetitive behavior

← — — — — — — — — — — — — — →

Most Severe | | | **Least Severe**

FIGURE 1.2. Autistic Disorder symptoms present along a continuum of severity. As one moves along this continuum (from left to right), symptoms have a reduced impact on adaptive functioning and the potential for independent functioning increases. These symptoms change over time, with IQ and language being the best predictors of movement from most to least severe. Adapted from Wing (1991).

impairment. As discussed earlier, children who receive intensive early intervention tend to have better outcomes than those who do not receive such intervention. In addition, children who have more severely delayed cognitive functioning and language tend to have a poorer outcome than do their peers without such delays (Mastergeorge, Rogers, Corbett, Solomon, 2003; Wing, 1995).

Asperger's Disorder. First described by Hans Asperger in 1944, the primary symptoms of Asperger's Disorder are "severe and sustained impairment in social interaction . . . and the development of restricted, repetitive patterns of behaviors, interests, and activities" (APA, 2000, p. 80). With the exception of not requiring symptoms of delayed communication [Asperger's Disorder criteria require "no clinically significant general delay in language" (p. 84)], the diagnostic criteria for Asperger's and Autistic Disorders are essentially the same. However, diagnosis requires that Autistic Disorder be ruled out before Asperger's Disorder is considered. Thus, it is not surprising that the rate of Asperger's is lower than that of Autistic Disorder.

Although early language skills are preserved, their circumscribed interests, about which they may speak incessantly, adversely affect the conversational reciprocity of children with Asperger's Disorder. In addition, they tend to make socially inappropriate statements and often sound like little professors, using unusual and sophisticated words. The rhythm, stress, and intonation (prosody) of their language are affected, and these children often speak in a monotone (Tidmarsh & Volkmar, 2003).

The cognitive functioning of individuals with Asperger's Disorder is much more homogeneous than that found among individuals with Autistic Disorder. Although individuals with Autistic Disorder are often cognitively impaired, the intellectual functioning of individuals with Asperger's Disorder is typically within normal limits. These individuals can complete high levels of education; however, their adult functioning is often adversely affected by their impaired social skills (APA, 2000; Tidmarsh & Volkmar, 2003).

It is important to note that the functional difference between Asperger's Disorder and *High Functioning* Autistic Disorder (i.e., those who meet the criteria for Autistic Disorder and who have IQs above 70) is not clear. There are no indications of the need for different treatment approaches for these two groups and the two are more alike than they are different (Ozonoff, Dawson, &, McPartland, 2000; Ozonoff & Rogers, 2003).

PDD-NOS. This classification is reserved for individuals who experience difficulty in at least two of the three Autistic Disorder symptom clusters but who do not meet the complete diagnostic criteria for any other PDD (APA, 2000). According to Filipek and colleagues (1999), PDD-NOS is not a distinct clinical entity. However, individuals with this diagnosis typically have milder symptoms.

It is important to acknowledge that the PDD-NOS diagnostic classification is sometimes employed when a diagnostician is simply reluctant to use the Autistic Disorder label. In fact, in one study 176 children with Autistic Disorder were judged to not be significantly different from 18 children with PDD-NOS on any neuropsychological or behavioral measure (when nonverbal IQ was controlled; Rapin et al., 1996; cited in Filipek et al., 1999).

Childhood Disintegrative Disorder. Also known as Heller's syndrome, Childhood Disintegrative Disorder is a very rare condition with a prevalence rate of 1.7 per 100,000. It is more likely to affect males. Like Autistic Disorder, it involves impaired development of social interaction and communication; and restricted, repetitive, and stereotyped patterns of behaviors, interests, and mannerisms. However, a distinct pattern of regression (occurring before 10 years of age) following at least two years of normal development distinguishes it from Autistic Disorder. This pattern includes the ubiquitous loss of speech and frequent deterioration of bladder/bowel and motor skills (Bray, Kehle, & Theodore, 2002; Malhotra & Gupta, 2002). Severe cognitive deficits are typically associated with Childhood Disintegrative Disorder (APA, 2000; Tidmarsh & Volkmar, 2003).

Rett's Disorder. With a prevalence rate of 1 per 20,000, Rett's Disorder is a progressive developmental disorder that occurs primarily among females. Examination of diagnostic criteria reveals that Rett's Disorder is relatively distinct. A pattern of head growth deceleration (between the ages of 5 and 48 months), a loss of purposeful hand skills, and the presence of awkward gait and trunk movement distinguish Rett's from the other PDDs. Because affected girls gradually lose gross motor function, motor delays and not language delays are often the initial referring concern. Although social difficulties characteristic of Autistic and Asperger's Disorders may be observed, they are not as pervasive and tend to be transient. In the later stages of the disorder (between 2 and 10 years) social skills improve. Severe to profound cognitive deficits are typically associated with Rett's Disorder. By adolescence, girls with this disorder have muscle wasting, scoliosis, spasticity, and decreased mobility (APA, 2000; Tidmarsh & Volkmar, 2003).

Regarding these latter two classifications (Childhood Disintegrative and Rett's Disorders), it is important to acknowledge that as researchers have come to understand more about them and their respective etiologies (particularly of Rett's Disorder), their relationship with other autism spectrum disorders has been called into question (Szatmari, 2004). In fact, Ozonoff and Rogers (2003) have speculated: "It is likely that these conditions will not be so closely associated with autism in the future and will be considered distinct neurodegenerative disorders (p. 11). Because of this unclear relationship between Rett's Disorder, CDD, and autism spectrum disorders, this book will emphasize research dealing with Autistic and Asperger's Disorders.

Autism and Special Education Eligibility

One of the more important intervention options to be considered by school professionals serving students with autism is special education services, and as was mentioned earlier in this chapter, the past decade has seen a dramatic increase in the number of students with autism receiving special education assistance. Thus, this book begins with an exploration of how school professionals can better identify and serve students with autism and a brief review of the topic of special education eligibility.

First, and foremost, it is critical to recognize that *DSM IV-TR* diagnoses are not synonymous with special education eligibility (Fogt et al., 2003; US Department of Education, 2000). According to proposed *Individuals with Disabilities Education Improvement Act* (IDEIA) 2004 regulations [US Department of Education, 2005 (c)(1)(i)], eligibility for special education services as a student with autism is defined as follows:

1. Autism means a developmental disability significantly affecting verbal and nonverbal communication and social interaction, generally evident before age three that adversely affects a child's educational performance. Other characteristics often associated with autism are engagement in repetitive activities and stereotypical movements, resistance to environmental change or change in daily routines, and unusual responses to sensory experiences.

   i. Autism does not apply if a child's educational performance is adversely affected primarily because the child has an emotional disturbance, as defined in paragraph (c)(4) of this section.

   ii. A child who manifests the characteristics of autism after age three could be identified as having autism if the criteria in paragraph (c)(1)(i) of this section are satisfied.

It has been argued that, given this eligibility classification statement, distinctions among the various *DSM IV-TR* PDDs may not be important. Specifically, Shriver, Allen, and Mathews (1999) suggest that for special education eligibility purposes, "the federal definition of 'autism' was written sufficiently broad to encompass children who exhibit a range of characteristics of autism such as PDD-NOS and Asperger's Disorder" (p. 539). However, Fogt and colleagues (2003) suggest that it is less clear if students with milder forms of autism would be eligible. In their review of published case law addressing the eligibility of students with autism for special education, Fogt and her colleagues observed that "adjudicative decision makers almost never use the *DSM IV-TR* criteria exclusively or primarily for determining whether the child is eligible as autistic" (p. 211). Although *DSM IV-TR* criteria were considered in just over half of the cases reviewed, all but one case acknowledged *IDEA* as the "controlling authority" (p. 211). Thus, when it comes to special education, it is state and federal education codes and regulations (not *DSM IV-TR*) that drive eligibility decisions. School professionals involved in making eligibility decisions for students with autism are advised by Fogt and her colleagues "to become thoroughly familiar with the diagnostic criteria for autism specified in the *IDEA* and to bear clearly in mind that the DSM definition is not legally controlling" (p. 211).

Given the *IDEA* requirement that autism must "adversely affect a child's education performance" before a given student can be found eligible, some generalizations about the likelihood that a specific autism spectrum disorder will result in special education eligibility can be made. First, given that a majority of students with Autistic Disorder are also mentally retarded (Fombonne, 1999), it should be expected that a majority of students with this diagnosis would also be eligible for special education under *IDEA* (Fogt, Miller, & Zirkel, 2003). However, the intellectual functioning of individuals with Asperger's Disorder is typically within the average range. Hence, it is suggested that students with Asperger's Disorder will require more careful examination by an Individual Educational Planning (IEP) team to determine if their learning needs necessitate special education assistance. Similarly, individuals with PDD-NOS and high functioning autism are typically viewed as having milder symptoms. Given this fact, these students may also require more careful examination by an IEP team to determine if their learning needs necessitate special education assistance. Finally, given the severe to profound cognitive deficits typically associated with Childhood Disintegrative and Rett's Disorders, it is expected that IEP teams will typically certify these students as eligible for special education assistance.

Purpose and Plan of This Book

In the pages that follow, school professionals are provided with the information they need to be better prepared to identify and address the needs of students with autism. Chapter 2 offers an exploration of the complex etiology of autism. In Chapter 3, epidemiological issues are reviewed. Included here will be a discussion of the changing rates of autism both in special education and in the general population. Chapters 4, 5, and 6 review information essential to identification and assessment, and, finally, Chapter 7 presents a summary of research examining the effectiveness of interventions for children with autism.

2
Causes

Researchers have been attempting to find the causes of autism since it was first identified by Kanner in 1943. Although Kanner initially suggested autism to have a biological basis; most early efforts to identify the causes of autism focused on inadequate nurturance by emotionally cold and indifferent parents (Ozonoff & Rogers, 2003). However, in the words of Ozonoff and Rogers (2003): "It is now abundantly clear that autism is a biological disorder and is not caused by parenting deficiencies or other social factors" (p. 18). Today, it is accepted that the behavioral manifestations of autism are a consequence of abnormal brain development, structure, and function. The brain structures implicated in autism are illustrated in Figure 2.1 (Strock, 2004).

Although it is clear that autism has an organic etiology, the underlying causes of these neurological differences, and exactly how they manifest themselves, is much more controversial. Literature reviews conducted by Muhle, Trentacoste, and Rapin (2004), Rapin and Katzman (1998), and Newschaffer, Fallin, and Lee (2002) suggest the etiology of autism to be complex and multifaceted, resulting from the interaction of genetic, neurological, and environmental factors. Specifically, it has been suggested that some combination of genetic predisposition(s) and gene by environmental interaction(s) result in the brain abnormalities, which in turn are the causes of the range of behaviors we currently refer to as autism spectrum behaviors. These hypothetical relationships are summarized in Figure 2.2.

Genetics

There is strong evidence that autism is heritable (Muhle et al., 2004). Ozonoff and Rogers (2003) suggest that there are four primary lines of research pointing to the role of genetic factors in autism. First, they refer to research that has documented a 3 to 6 percent increased risk for autism among the siblings of children with an autism spectrum disorder, a rate that far exceeds that found in the general population. Second, they site research that has found that if one identical twin has Autistic Disorder, 60 percent of the time the other twin will also have this condition. This percentage jumps to 90 percent when both twins are viewed from

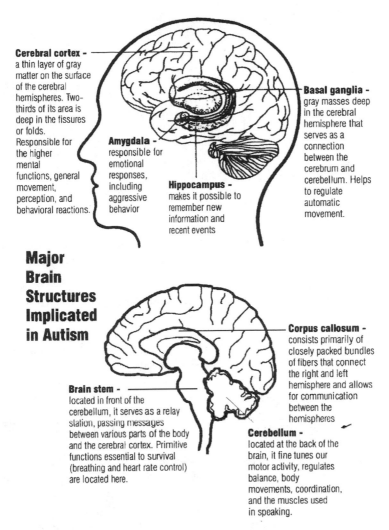

Cerebral cortex - a thin layer of gray matter on the surface of the cerebral hemispheres. Two-thirds of its area is deep in the fissures or folds. Responsible for the higher mental functions, general movement, perception, and behavioral reactions.

Amygdala - responsible for emotional responses, including aggressive behavior

Hippocampus - makes it possible to remember new information and recent events

Basal ganglia - gray masses deep in the cerebral hemisphere that serves as a connection between the cerebrum and cerebellum. Helps to regulate automatic movement.

Major Brain Structures Implicated in Autism

Brain stem - located in front of the cerebellum, it serves as a relay station, passing messages between various parts of the body and the cerebral cortex. Primitive functions essential to survival (breathing and heart rate control) are located here.

Corpus callosum - consists primarily of closely packed bundles of fibers that connect the right and left hemisphere and allows for communication between the hemispheres

Cerebellum - located at the back of the brain, it fine tunes our motor activity, regulates balance, body movements, coordination, and the muscles used in speaking.

FIGURE 2.1. The brain structures implicated in autism. [Reprinted from Margaret Strock (2004), *Autism Spectrum Disorders*. Bethesda, MD: NIMH (p. 29). This work is in the public domain.]

the perspective of the broader autism spectrum. Conversely, among fraternal twins (who have developed from two separate ova), the risk of both twins having autism is no greater than that found among non-twin siblings.

Third, Ozonoff and Rogers (2003) acknowledge research that has documented autism to be associated with a variety of genetic and chromosomal abnormalities. However, it is important to note that current estimates suggest that less than 10 percent of all autism cases are caused by a diagnosable medical condition, chromosomal abnormality, or genetic defect (e.g., tuberous sclerosis, fragile X;

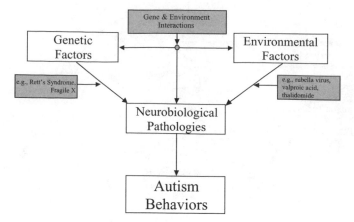

FIGURE 2.2. The hypothetical relationships between genetics, the environment, and the brain abnormalities that are the likely causes of autism.

Muhle et al., 2004). Finally, they cite research suggesting that besides autism, the families of individuals with autism tend to demonstrate a set of cognitive and social differences that are not seen in other family groups. Although these data are very powerful, at present the identity and number of genes associated with autism is not known and is the focus of much scientific inquiry.

Identification of Autism Genes

The human genome is composed of 23 pairs of chromosomes (numbered 1 to 22, with X and Y designating the sex chromosomes). Combinations of 30,000 to 40,000 different genes form each chromosome. Composed of deoxyribonucleic acid (DNA), genes function as blueprints for growth and development. If a particular gene is changed in some way, its ability to direct normal development is affected. Similarly, if a chromosome is damaged in some way, it can affect normal development by altering the numerous genes located in that part of the chromosome (Exploring Autism, 2002; The National Autistic Society, 2004). To better understand the genetics of autism, researchers currently employ several different methods. Muhle and colleagues (2004) divide these methods into: (a) cytogenetic studies, (b) genome searches, and (c) candidate gene searches.

Cytogenetic studies. This type of research examines chromosome number and/or structure to identify abnormalities that may be associated with autism. Using various viewing techniques, researchers examine the chromosomes of individuals with autism and search for visible breakpoints, translocations, duplications, and deletions (Exploring Autism, 2002). When such abnormalities are found, the hunt for specific autism genes within that region begins. Muhle and colleagues (2004) suggest that among individuals with autism, abnormalities are "fairly frequent" on chromosome 15 (15q) (p. 472). Currently it is speculated that there are at least

TABLE 2.1. Genes suspected to be involved in autism.

Gene(s)	Chromosome(s)
5-hydroxytryptamine (serotonin) transporter (*5HTT*) gene	17
Gamma-aminobutyric acid A receptor b3 (*GABRB3*) gene	15
Reelin (*RELN*) gene	7
Homeobox (*HOX*) genes	7, 17, 2
Fragile X genes	X
C-Harvey-ras (*HRAS*) gene	11

Sources: Muhle et al. (2004) and Newschaffer et al. (2002).

22 chromosome regions containing genes associated with autism (Xu, Zwaigenbaum, Szatmari, & Scherer, 2004). It is important to note that while cytogenetic studies are helpful in identifying regions of interest in and of themselves, these techniques cannot identify the specific genes that may cause autism.

Genome searches. This type of research examines the genetic material of families that include individuals with autism. Within these families, DNA sequences (or markers) along different chromosomes are examined by researchers for slight differences (referred to as polymorphisms). Researchers then try to find differences that are consistently found among family members who have autism, but not among those without the disorder. By determining how close the polymorphism, unique to the autism family members, are to a specific gene (done via statistical methods), the polymorphism can be "linked" to that gene (Exploring Autism, 2002). When such linkages are made, the hunt for a specific autism gene within that chromosome region begins. Muhle and colleagues (2004) suggest that at least 10 different genes have been associated with autism using this technique, with the putative speech and language region (7q31–q33) "most strongly linked with autism" (p. 472). Here again it should be noted that these studies are helpful in identifying chromosomal regions of interest. However, linking a given polymorphism and a given gene does not mean that a specific gene has been found. Rather, it means that it is likely that such a gene is nearby.

Candidate gene searches. This research begins with the assumption that certain specific genes are likely to be associated with autism. These prior assumptions are based upon clinical and empirical evidence (including whole genome searches and cytogenetic analysis) that a specific gene is associated with the development of specific autism symptoms. Using this method, several research teams have found associations between autism and at least six different genes or gene groups. These genes are listed in Table 2.1. However, there has been no consistent replication of positive findings for any of these genes (Newschaffer et al., 2002).

Concluding Comments Regarding the Role of Genetics

It is not likely that autism is a purely genetic disorder (Ozonoff & Rogers, 2003). With the exception of Rett's Syndrome [which is caused in the majority of cases by changes to a gene on the X chromosome (Xq28)], there is no conclusive evidence that autism is associated with any specific genetic defect. Rather, the available data suggests that multiple genetic factors cause a majority of cases of autism (Muhle et al., 2004). Models of how this might work include an additive threshold model (wherein a certain number of factors are needed to reach a critical threshold for autism to develop) and an epistatic model (wherein multiple predisposing genes interact with each other to cause autism; Newschaffer et al., 2002). Also yet to be identified are the potential environmental and biological triggers that may interact with these genetic predispositions and result in the symptoms defined as autism.

Environment

Among family members (including identical twins), the manifestations of autism can vary substantially. This fact strongly argues that simple models of inheritance do not account for this spectrum of disorders (London & Etzel, 2000) and has facilitated a recent increase in studies of possible environmental factors in autism. This line of study is reinforced by prior research documenting that environmental factors (e.g., alcohol) can cause developmental disabilities (e.g., fetal alcohol syndrome). However, to the extent the environment does have a role in causing autism, it has been suggested that it does so by interacting with certain genes. Thus, a certain gene or gene combinations may generate a susceptibility to autism that is in turn triggered by a certain environmental factor or factors (Newschaffer et al., 2002). Environmental factors currently being considered include obstetric suboptimality, prenatal, and postnatal factors.

Obstetric Suboptimality

According to Newschaffer and colleagues (2002), the combination of evidence suggesting autism to have its origins in prenatal development and the lack of any specific factor as being the cause of autism has led to the study of summary measures of the pregnancy and delivery's "optimality" (e.g., maternal age, maternal disease, neonatal respiratory distress). Most studies that have considered obstetric suboptimality have found lower optimality among children with autism when compared with normal controls (Glasson et al., 2004; Newschaffer et al., 2002). However, whether this is a cause or a consequence of autism remains unknown, and Hansen and Hagerman (2003) suggest that these variables "... likely represent additive brain trauma to a vulnerable child rather than a distinct etiology of ASD" (p. 99).

Prenatal Factors

Maternal infection and drug exposure are two prenatal factors reported by Newschaffer and colleagues (2002) as having been the focus of prior study. Regarding the former, rubella has been specifically associated with autism. However,

Newschaffer et al. conclude: "The low frequency of reports suggests that infectious diseases known to be associated with neuropathology are not a major independent cause of ASD" (p. 145). Cytomegalovirus, herpes, and HIV have also been associated with autism (Hansen & Hagerman, 2003).

Regarding drug exposure, taking thalidomide during the 20th to 24th weeks of pregnancy has been correlated with an increased risk of autistic disorder (Miller & Stömland, 1999). Valproic acid (know by the brand names Depakene and Depakote) and alcohol abuse have also been suggested to increase the risk of autism (Hansen & Hagerman, 2003; Newschaffer et al., 2002).

Postnatal Factors

Herpes encephalitis and other infections (e.g., chickenpox) have been associated with autism. However, current research does not support the potential etiological role of chemical exposures, the measles-mumps-rubella vaccine, nor mercury and thimerosal-containing vaccines (Newschaffer et al., 2002). Epidemiological data from the US and Europe have not found relationships between thimerosal nor vaccines and autism. According to the Institute of Medicine's Immunization Safety Review Committee (2004), ". . . the evidence favors rejection of a causal relationship between thimerosal-containing vaccines and autism" (p. 16), and ". . . that the evidence favors rejection of a causal relationship between MMR vaccine and autism" (p. 16). Finally, Matsuishi and colleagues (1999) report that children with autistic disorder have a significantly higher incidence of meconium aspiration syndrome, which is associated with fetal hypoxia, when compared with the children in the control group. Again, it is not clear if the association is a cause or consequence associated with the development of autism.

Concluding Comments Regarding the Role of the Environment

Currently, there is very little evidence supporting any one environmental factor as playing a primary role in the development of autism. Thus, to the extent environmental factors (both those that affect the mother and those that affect the child who develops autism) are playing a causal role in the development of autism, it seems likely that they interact with a variety of genetic factors (both those carried by the mother and those carried by the child who will develop autism). The relationships between the environments of the mother and the child and the genetics of both is illustrated in Figure 2.3, which offers the model of potential etiologic effects put forward by Newschaffer and colleagues (2002).

Neurobiology

Contemporary scholars generally agree that autism's behavioral abnormalities are the result of developmental brain pathologies (Akshoomoff, Pierce, & Courchesne, 2002; Courchesne, Carper, & Akshoomoff, 2003; Newschaffer et al.,

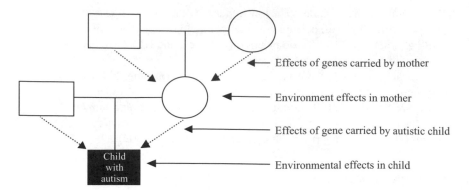

FIGURE 2.3. A model of the potential etiologic role of the environments of the mother and the child, and the genetics of both mother and child. [Reprinted from Newschaffer et al., "Heritable and Nonheritable Risk Factors for Autism Spectrum Disorders, *Epidemiologic Review*, 2002, 24(2), 137–153, by permission of Oxford University Press. Copyright © 2002 Johns Hopkins Bloomberg School of Public Health.]

2002; Nicolson & Szatmari, 2003). No single pathology has been found to account for all cases of autism, rather several different etiologies have been proposed. This fact is consistent with the hypothesis that autism is not a distinct clinical entity. Rather, it is a collection of different disorders with similar behavioral manifestations.

Brain Size

Clinical onset of autism's behavioral manifestations appears to be preceded by slightly reduced head size at birth, followed by a rapid and excessive increase in head circumference measurements (reported to be an accurate index of early brain size) between 1 to 2 and 6 to 14 months. Although seen in 6 percent of healthy developing infants, Courchesne and colleagues (2003) found 59 percent of the 48 children they studied to demonstrate such growth. They report that on average, between 6 to 14 months head size increased from the 25th to the 84th percentile rank (according to CDC norms). These data are illustrated in Figure 2.4. Especially provocative was the finding that the most dramatic early increases in head size were demonstrated among those children with more severe Autistic Disorder. Conversely, those with less severe manifestations of autism (e.g., PDD-NOS) showed smaller increases. This rapid early growth in the first year of life is then followed by a period of two to four years during which the rate of brain growth slows, and then during middle or late childhood through adolescence a plateau in overall head growth occurs.

Given that the first year of life is an important period of brain development and learning, Courchesne and colleagues (2003) speculate that this early period of rapid brain growth is an important causal factor in the emergence of autistic symptoms.

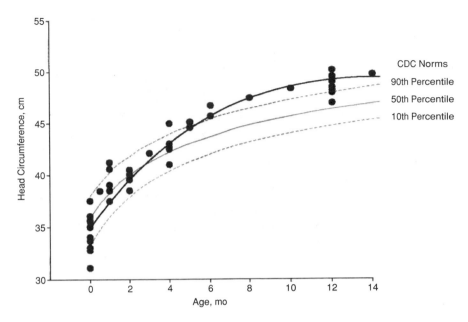

FIGURE 2.4. Courchesne et al. (2003, p. 342) head circumference measurements for a sample of children with autism as compared to CDC norms. [Reprinted from *JAMA* with permission from the American Medical Association. Copyright © 2003 American Medical Association.]

They suggest that this rapid and disordered growth "produces in too short a time too many [synaptic] connections that may not be adaptive. Faced with the neural noise that would be the result of such rapidly changing aberrant connections, the infant would lose the ability to make sense of its world and withdraw" (p. 343, word in brackets added).

MRI data from a study by Akshoomoff and colleagues (2004) confirm that brain size is a correlate of autism among preschool-age children. In this study, the brains of 52 boys with a provisional diagnosis of autism (aged 1.9 to 5.2 years) and 15 typically developing children (aged 1.7 to 5.2 years) were measured via MRI technology. Subsequently, after the age of 5 years, diagnostic and cognitive testing allowed the autism group to be divided into low functioning (*n* = 30), high functioning (verbal and non-verbal IQs of at least 70, *n* = 12), and PDD-NOS (met *DSM-IV* criteria, but did not meet diagnostic test cutoffs for autism, *n* = 10) groups. This allowed for comparisons of the previously obtained MRI data not only between autism and typically developing children, but also for comparisons among the children with autism spectrum disorders.

Results revealed significant differences in brain size among the groups. For the low-functioning autism group, whole brain, overall cerebral, cerebral gray matter, cerebellar white matter volumes, and the anterior cerebellar vermis area were significantly larger than that found in the control group. For the high-functioning autism and PDD-NOS groups, cerebellar white matter volumes and the anterior cerebellar vermis area were significantly larger than that found in the control group. In addition, the low-functioning and high-functioning autism groups had significantly different posterior cerebellar vermis areas, with the low-functioning group mean size being significantly smaller than the high-functioning mean. Discriminant function analysis[1] (using cerebellar white and gray matter volumes, area of the anterior and posterior cerebellar vermis, and cerebral white and gray matter volumes as predictors of group membership) correctly classified 84.6 percent of the low-functioning group, 66.7 percent of the high-functioning group, 10 percent of the PDD-NOS group, and all but one (92.3 percent) of the control group. From these data, Akshoomoff and colleagues (2004) conclude that neuroanatomical measures discriminate children with autism from typically developing children. In addition, they suggest that the "results also demonstrate that there are neuroanatomical differences between young children with autism who are higher functioning compared to those who are lower functioning" (p. 355).

Brain Structure

From a review of the literature, Akshoomoff and colleagues (2002) suggest that there is strong evidence for neuroanatomical abnormalities among children with autism (see Figure 2.1). Specifically, they point to postmortem and MRI research that has documented that among individuals with autism, most major brain structures are affected. These areas include the hippocampus and amygdala, cerebellum, cerebral cortex, limbic system, corpus callosum, basal ganglia, and brain stem (Tharp, 2003).

Casanova, Buxhoeveden, Switala, and Roy (2002) have described what may be the most fundamental structural anomalies in the brains of individuals with autism. In a postmortem study, the brains of nine individuals with autism (mean age 12 years) were compared with the brains of nine control subjects (mean age 15 years). Results revealed that individuals with autism differed from normally developing people in the size, number, and arrangement of minicolumns in the prefrontal cortex and in the temporal lobe. Minicolumns are considered to be the basic anatomical and physiological unit of the brain; they take in, process, and then respond to stimuli (Buxhoeveden & Casanova, 2002). Casanova has compared minicolumns to information processing computer chips (McKinney, 2002).

Using computerized imaging software to obtain cell measurements, Casanova and colleagues (2002) found the autistic group's minicolumns to be narrower than those found among the normal control group. Specifically, the autistic group's minicolumns were more numerous, smaller, and less compact in their arrangement (i.e., the cells were more dispersed) than those found among the control group. Figure 2.5 provides images that illustrate these differences.

---

[1] Discriminant function analysis is a statistical technique that can be used to predict group membership. It uses a combination of variables (in this case specific measures of brain size) to predict group membership.

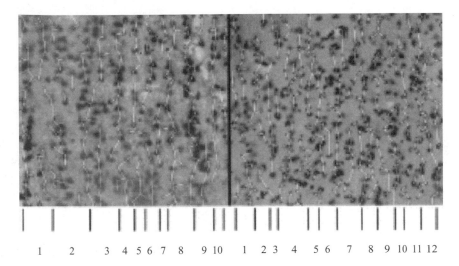

FIGURE 2.5. Casanova et al.'s (2002, p. 431) microscopic fields (original magnification × 100) analysis of layer III of temporoparietal auditory area from the brain of an individual with autism (right) and an age-matched control (left): The superimposed white lines indicate the cell core of the minicolumn. Lines and numbers at the bottom of each figure define the boundaries of each minicolumn. [Reprinted from the American Association of Neurology's journal *Neurology,* with permission from Lippincott Williams & Wilkins. Copyright © 2002 Lippincott Williams & Wilkins.]

The authors speculate that the extra minicolumns may result in cortical "noise" (p. 431). They further suggest that their findings are consistent with the view that autism is a disorder of the brain's arousal-modulating systems and that due to the extra minicolumns ". . . autistic individuals experience a chronic state of overarousal and exhibit abnormal behaviors to diminish this arousal" (p. 431). If correct, this hypothesis may help to explain some of the behavioral abnormalities observed among individuals with autism. For example, difficulty establishing and maintaining eye contact may be a consequence of being overpowered by the stimuli received when looking someone in the eye (McKinney, 2002).

Brain Chemistry

Through comprehensive literature reviews, Ciaranello and Cirananello (1995) and Rapin and Katzman (1998) identified factors that have been implicated consistently in the development of autism. Their examination of evidence for neurochemical bases for autism reveals a consistent association only with elevated serotonin levels, which are found in the blood of about 25 percent of individuals with autism. Special relevance to autism may be found in the fact that serotonin is involved in the formation of new neurons in the brain ("neurogenesis") and is thought to be important in the regulation of "neuronal differentiation, synaptogenesis, and neuronal migration during development" (Newschaffer et al., 2002, p. 138). Supporting this hypothesis that abnormal serotonin metabolism is common among individuals with autism is the finding that depletion of tryptophan (a precursor of serotonin) in the diet worsens the behavior of a substantial percentage of children with autism (Joshi, Percy, & Brown, 2004).

It has also been suggested that the inhibition of gamma-aminobutyric acid (GABA) may contribute to the specific functional deficits in autism (e.g., impaired ability to process sensory information and learning tasks). Hussman (2001) proposed a hypothesis of suppressed GABAergic inhibition in autism, which results in excessive stimulation of glutamate-specialized neurons and loss of sensory gating. It is suggested that these hypotheses of impaired neurotransmission in autism are consistent with a broad range of findings from other neurochemical and neuroanatomic research.

Concluding Comments Regarding the Role of Neurobiology

Newschaffer and colleagues (2002) conclude that the variety of different neuropathologies associated with autism implies that these disorders have a variety of different causes. Although these authors argue that these brain differences likely have a prenatal origin, they acknowledge that the plasticity associated with the young brain ". . . may still allow for postnatal factors to affect the disease's natural history" (p. 138).

Concluding Comments

This chapter has illustrated the complexity of the issue of autism's causes. Despite the multitude of research exploring its etiology, definitive conclusions regarding the causes of autism remain elusive. A problem of particular importance relates to the wide range of manifestations of autism symptomatology: two children (even identical twins) diagnosed with autism falling at different points of the autism spectrum may share few characteristics. Consequently, conclusive findings of a single cause for autism are most unlikely. The current consensus regarding the cause of autism is provided in a multifaceted model, which includes genetic, neurobiological, and neuroanatomical mechanisms, as well as environmental influences. In order to successfully integrate findings of several approaches, further research is needed to clarify the nature of the complex interplay between different mechanisms and their unique contribution to the development of autism.

3
Prevalence and Associated Conditions

As mentioned in Chapter 1, recent epidemiological studies have suggested that the incidence of autism is increasing. According to Fombonne (2003b), the best current estimate of autism's prevalence is approximately 60 per 10,000. In schools, the increased incidence of autism is demonstrated by the increasing numbers of students classified as autistic and served under the *Individuals with Disabilities Education Act* (IDEA; US Department of Education, 2003). This chapter provides a review of research that has examined the incidence of autism (both in special education and the general population) and explores arguments that attempt to account for recent increases in the rates of these disorders. In addition, research is presented that has documented autism's association with other conditions.

Students with Autism Served Under IDEA

Although the education of children with autism was accepted as a public responsibility as part of the Education Act of All Handicapped Children in 1975, it was not until 1991 that the US Department of Education added autism as a specific special education eligibility category. Since that time, the number of children classified for special education purposes as autistic has steadily increased. From data provided by the US Department of Education (2005), Figure 3.1 illustrates the increase in the number of students falling in this special education eligibility classification. In 2004 there were a total of 165,552 school-aged students (6 to 21 years of age) with autism served under *IDEA*, most of whom (96,799) were 6- to 11-years-old. Taking into account increases in the population of all students served under *IDEA*, Figure 3.2 illustrates that autism, as a percentage of students in special education, is also increasing. In 2004, students classified with autism represented 2.7 percent of all school-age students with disabilities served under *IDEA* (up from .001 percent in 1991). Table 3.1 also summarizes these data.

However, further analysis of US Department of Education (2004) data suggests the possibility that the increasing number of students with autism in the special education population is not indicative of a true increase in these disorders. Specifically, it might be argued that autism classifications have been substituted for other

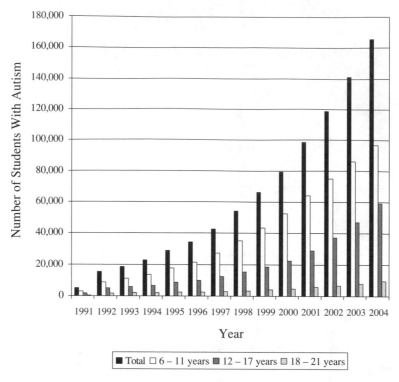

FIGURE 3.1. The number of students with autism served under *IDEA* by age group and year: 1991 through 2004. [*Source*: U.S. Department of Education (2005).]

eligibility classifications such as mental retardation. For example, it is possible that instead of labeling students as mentally retarded, IEP teams may instead be classifying them as eligible for special education under autism criteria. In support of this hypothesis, Table 3.2 documents and Figure 3.3 illustrates that as the incidence of autism classification has increased, the incidence of mental retardation has decreased. Whereas the number of students with autism, as a percentage of all students with disabilities served under *IDEA* increased by 2.6 percent between 1991 and 2004, the number eligible under the mental retardation criteria during this same time period has decreased by almost the same amount (minus 2.8 percent).

A potential explanation for the changes in autism and mental retardation rates is that IEP teams have become better able to identify students with autism and that a percentage of students with mental retardation were previously misclassified. Another explanation for this classification substitution might be found in the authors' observation that the diagnosis of autism is more acceptable in today's schools than is the diagnosis of mental retardation. Whereas the later diagnosis has a fairly uniform (and typically poor) prognosis, the diagnosis of autism appears to be viewed by many of today's school professionals (and parents) as having the potential for more positive outcomes. In addition, the intensive early intervention services often made available to students with autism are not always offered to the child whose

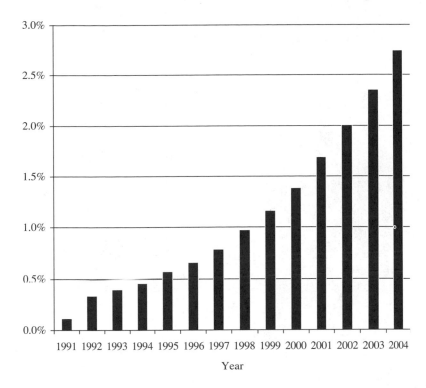

FIGURE 3.2. Students with autism served under *IDEA* by year as a percentage of all students with disabilities: 1991 through 2004. [*Source*: U.S. Department of Education (2005).]

primary eligibility classification is mental retardation. Thus, IEP teams may be especially motivated to identify students as eligible for *IDEA* services under the autism criteria.

Finally, it is important to acknowledge that the rate of autism in the general population is much greater than *IDEA* data suggests. This is primarily due to the fact that *IDEA* data do not include those students with autism who have been determined eligible for services under another eligibility category (e.g., mental retardation, speech and language impairment) and preschool age children with autism. Specifically, it appears that just over 40 percent of children with autism are classified as such under *IDEA* (Yeargin-Allsopp, 2003). While it is estimated that there are more then 300,000 children ages 5 to 17 years with autism in the US(Fombonne, 2003b), there were only approximately 133,000 children ages 6 to 17 years classified as autistic under *IDEA* in 2003 (US Department of Education, 2003). In addition, as mentioned in Chapter 1, it is expected that some children with milder forms of autism (i.e., Asperger's Disorder and high-functioning Autistic Disorder) will not require special education assistance (their autism will not have an adverse effect on their educational performance) and their numbers are not represented in these data. In a recent study of the prevalence of autism, Yeargin-Allsopp and colleagues

TABLE 3.1. Number of students with autism served under *IDEA* by age group and year (1991 through 2004)

Age Group	1991	1992	1993	1994	1995	1996	1997	1998	1999	2000	2001	2002	2003	2004
6–11 years	2,896	8,769	10,981	13,538	17,477	21,469	27,154	34,938	43,292	52,172	63,794	74,446	85,577	96,799
12–17 years	1,613	4,789	5,702	6,648	8,685	9,965	12,069	15,326	18,359	22,329	28,668	37,154	46,837	59,253
18–21 years	585	1,744	2,013	2,145	2,563	2,574	2,914	3,380	3,966	4,584	5,570	6,669	7,986	9,500
Total Autism	5,094	15,302	18,696	22,331	28,725	34,008	42,137	53,664	65,617	79,085	98,032	118,269	140,400	165,552
All Disabilities	4,464,761	4,592,790	4,736,029	4,866,540	5,036,139	5,185,444	5,347,058	5,486,630	5,620,764	5,711,482	5,797,930	5,892,878	5,970,497	6,033,425
% with Autism	.114	.333	.395	.459	.570	.656	.788	.978	1.167	1.385	1.691	2.007	2.325	2.744

Source: US Department of Education (2005).

TABLE 3.2. Number of students with autism and students with mental retardation served under *IDEA* by age group and year (1991 through 2004)

	1991	1992	1993	1994	1995	1996	1997	1998	1999	2000	2001	2002	2003	2004
Total Autism	5,094	15,302	18,696	22,331	28,725	34,008	42,137	53,664	65,617	79,085	98,032	118,269	140,400	165,552
% with Autism[a]	.114	.333	.395	.459	.570	.656	.788	.978	1.167	1.385	1.691	2.007	2.325	2.744
Total MR	537,602	518,498	536,632	555,440	570,825	579,509	589,093	596,824	600,457	599,738	592,657	580,656	571,124	555,524
% with MR[a]	12.041	11.289	11.331	11.413	11.335	11.176	11.017	10.878	10.638	10.501	10.22	9.854	9.566	9.207
All Disabilities	4,464,761	4,592,790	4,736,029	4,866,540	5,036,139	5,185,444	5,347,058	5,486,630	5,620,764	5,711,482	5,797,930	5,892,878	5,970,497	6,033,425

Source: US Department of Education (2005).
Note: [a]When compared to the total number of students found eligible for special education under all *IDEA* eligibility categories.

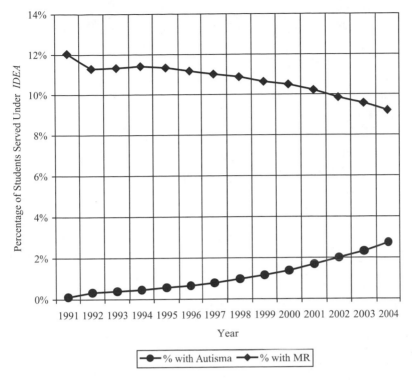

FIGURE 3.3. Students with autism or mental retardation served under *IDEA* by year as a percentage of all students with disabilities: 1991 through 2004. [*Source*: US Department of Education (2005).]

(2003) found that 9 percent of those identified as children with autism did not receive special education services at the time of the study (1996). These data suggest that the number of students with autism is greater than might be suggested by the rate of children classified as autistic under *IDEA* criteria.

Changes in Autism Rates in the General Population

Fombonne (2003a) recently reviewed autism prevalence data obtained from 32 separate studies. He reports that due to methodological differences (e.g., different case finding, population sampling), these studies yielded rates of Autistic Disorder that varied significantly. From data obtained since 1987, he concluded that the best estimate for Autistic Disorder was 10 per 10,000. Relatively few of the studies reviewed (n = 12) provided data on the other autism spectrum disorders. From these data, he estimated the prevalence rate of PDD-NOS to be 15 per 10,000 and Asperger's Disorder to be approximately 2.5 per 10,000. Combined, a conservative estimate of 27.5 per 10,000 was suggested for all autism spectrum disorders.

However, Fombonne also notes that several of the most recent studies (all published since 2000) were more methodologically sound, have examined the broader autism spectrum, and have generated prevalence rates ranging from 57.9 to 67.5 per 10,000! Fombonne suggest these rates to converge at approximately 60 per 10,000. Given these data, it has been suggested that the number of children identified with autism has significantly increased. The causes of this increased incidence, however, are a source of much debate (Fombonne, 2003, September).

A variety of explanations for the increasing rates of autism have been offered. At present, debate continues regarding whether the prevalence of autism has actually increased, or if prior data underestimated the true prevalence (Yeargin-Allsopp et al., 2003). From a review of the current literature, the most frequently made arguments are summarized below.

Changes in diagnostic criteria. The initial studies of the incidence of autism (e.g., Lotter, 1967) employed a rather narrow definition of autism (classic or Kanner's autism), one that is more closely aligned with what is currently labeled Autistic Disorder. Thus, one of the more common explanations for the increased rate of autism is the fact that different studies have used different definitions, and that the more current studies have employed a broader, more inclusive, definition (American Academy of Pediatrics, 2001; Barbaresi, Katusic, Colligan, Weaver, & Jacobsen, 2005; Barton & Volkmar, 1998; Chakrabarti & Fombonne, 2001; Fombonne, 2003, September; Gernsbacher, Dawson, & Goldsmith, 2005; Gillberg & Wing, 1999; Magnusson & Saemundsen, 2001). For example, Magnusson and Saemundsen (2001) examined the prevalence of autism in Iceland in two consecutive cohorts (participants born in 1974–1983 and in 1984–1993). According to the *International Classification of Diseases* (ICD) criteria, three diagnostic categories, Infantile autism (IA), Childhood autism (CA), and Atypical autism (AA), were included. The older cohort (1974–1983) was assessed with *ICD-9* and the younger cohort (1984–1993) with *ICD-10*. Results yielded a higher prevalence rate of autism in the younger cohort, with the rate of the older cohort being consistent with the range typically found in studies using Kanner's definition of autism and published prior to 1985 (4 to 5 per 10,000). The authors concluded that the apparent increase in the incidence of autism over time is a reflection of changes in diagnostic practices.

In another study, Gillberg and Wing (1999) reviewed all English language articles ever published on the prevalence of autism to determine if there has been a real increase in autism. Results indicate that early studies, from the 1960s and 1970s, suggested prevalence rates of under 0.5 per 1,000 children, whereas later studies from the 1980s to the present contained a mean rate of approximately 1 in 1,000 children. Interestingly, the only two US studies published on autism prevalence (1987 and 1989) reported atypically low rates, with prevalence being estimated at 3.4 in every 10,000 individuals. Among the suggestions provided by the authors for the increased autism prevalence was that using Kanner's original criteria provides significantly lower prevalence rates than if the *DSM* or *ICD* criteria are used. However, Gillberg and Wing conclude by suggesting that their review of prevalence studies does not resolve the question of whether or not the increase in autism is real.

In a recent editorial, Fombonne (2003b) observed that the rates of Autistic Disorder in the most recent surveys have consistently been significantly higher than earlier estimates. He concludes that from the available data that recent rates for both the broader autism spectrum and the narrower Autistic Disorder "are 3 to 4 times higher than 30 years ago" (p. 88). Thus, changes in diagnostic schemes alone would not appear to explain the increased rates of autism.

Heightened public awareness of autism. Another explanation for the increased prevalence of autism is that there is a heightened public awareness (and related media coverage) of these disorders, and as such caregivers are more likely to recognize and refer children with autism than they were in years past (Barbaresi et al., 2005; Chakrabarti & Fombonne, 2001; Gernsbacher et al., 2005; Yeargin-Allsopp et al., 2003). Gillberg and Wing (1999) put forward this possibility and suggested that the prevalence of autism has always been higher than earlier studies reported.

Increased willingness and ability to diagnosis autism. A third explanation for increased autism rates is that health care professionals (such as pediatricians and school psychologists) are better prepared and more willing to identify these disorders than they were previously (American Academy of Pediatrics, 2001; Chakrabarti & Fombonne, 2001; Gernsbacher et al., 2005; National Research Council, 2001; Yeargin-Allsopp et al., 2003). Thus, it may be that health care professionals are simply doing a better job of identifying children with autism (Fombonne, 2003, September).

One recent study that offered this explanation was authored by Powell and colleagues (2000). These researchers studied the changing incidence rates of autism in two regions of the United Kingdom between 1991 and 1996. Both classical childhood autism (most similar to what is now referred to as Autistic Disorder) and other autism spectrum disorders were studied. Cases of other disorders on the autism spectrum were detected from examination of records of child development centers and a regional child psychiatric referral center. Results suggested a male to female ratio of 6:1; and a rate of 8.3 per 10,000 for all children with autism spectrum disorders, 3.5 for classical autism, and 4.8 for other autism spectrum disorders. Rates for classical autism increased by 18 percent per year and rates for other autism spectrum disorders increased by 55 percent per year. The authors conclude that clinicians are becoming increasingly willing and able to diagnose autism spectrum disorders among preschool children.

Availability of resources for children with autism. A fourth explanation for increased autism rates is increased availability of resources for children with autism. For example, since 1991 autism has been an *IDEA* special education eligibility classification. Given the resources that accompany special education eligibility, it has been argued that the creation of this eligibility category helps, at least in part, to explain increased rates of this disorder. In other words, it has provided an important motivation for identifying students as children with autism. In addition, the mandate for early intervention services for children with developmental disabilities (such as autism), combined with the fact that children with autism respond well to early and intensive intervention (National Research Council, 2001), has likely served to further increase motivation to identify students with autism (Barbaresi et al., 2005; Yeargin-Allsopp, 2003).

In addition, representing and facilitating increased autism resources are the many advocacy groups that have been formed to assist children with autism and their families cope with these disorders (Yeargin-Allsopp et al., 2003). For a listing of some of these resources, the reader is referred to the Appendix.

Yet to be identified environmental factors. The combined influence of all of the factors listed above has likely contributed to the increased prevalence of children with autism (Yeargin-Allsopp et al., 2003). However, the increased incidence of these disorders is consistent with the possibility that environmental factors may be playing a role in the prevalence of autism (Frombonne, 2003b; 2003, September). Supporting this hypothesis is the Report to the Legislature (2002). This research project investigated reports of a 273 percent increase in reported cases of autism in California during the time period 1987 to 1998. To study this increase, a statewide sample of children from two birth year cohorts (1983–1985 and 1993–1995) were identified and data collected from the families of 375 children with a diagnosis of autism and 309 children with a diagnosis of mental retardation without autism. From the obtained data, it was concluded that there was no evidence that changes in demographics, the frequency of appropriate diagnoses, or diagnostic criteria alone contributed to the increased rate of autism. Thus, the study did not find evidence that the increased numbers of children identified as autistic could be attributed completely to artificial factors (i.e., loosening of diagnostic criteria for autism, more misclassification of autism, increased migration of children with autism to California). Without evidence of an artificial increase in autism cases, it was concluded that "some, if not all, of the observed increase represents a true increase in cases of autism in California" (p. 42). However, as Fombonne (2003b) points out, this report acknowledges that:

Improved case finding could result in an apparent increase in the number of cases of autism in California . . . . This study does not examine the extent to which differences in case finding over time have resulted in any changes in the number of autistic children who present to the Regional Centers. (p. 13)

Interestingly, analysis of the same data by Croen, Grether, Hoogstrate, & Selvin (2002) suggested that "diagnostic substitution" of autism for mental retardation explains the increase in autism rates. Their interpretation of the data suggested that to a significant extent the increase in autism rates might be explained by a decrease in the use of the diagnosis of mental retardation. Although the possibility that the rate of autism is in fact increasing cannot be ruled out, Fombonne (2003b) concluded that the evidence for a causal association between environmental factors and autism is "weak" (p. 88).

Autism's Correlates and Association with Other Conditions

Although it has been suggested that the overall proportion of cases of autism that can be causally attributed to known medical disorders is very low (Fombonne, 1999), autism has several different correlates and is frequently associated with a variety of other conditions. Although a source of some controversy, it has been suggested that up to 60 percent of children with autism have other medical and neurological disorders (Nordin & Gilberg, 1996; Yeargin-Allsopp et al., 2003). Ritvo and colleagues (1990), who conducted an epidemiological survey of autism in Utah, reported that the diseases known to produce pathology in the central nervous system are more prevalent in autistic populations.

Barton and Volkmar (1998) discussed the conflicting rates of autism's association with other medical conditions. They utilized a retrospective study to determine the prevalence of associated medical conditions and the resulting variability based on the systems used to diagnose autism. Criteria used to diagnose autism were based on either the *DSM-III* or the *DSM-III-R*. The authors conclude that differences in findings of previous research may be the result of the diagnostic system employed and which medical conditions are considered significant in the etiology of autism. Specifically, the broader diagnostic criteria typically results in the overdiagnosis of autism, particularly among those more severely disabled. Furthermore, it is among more severely disabled individuals that more medical conditions are found.

The remainder of this section explores specific conditions associated with autism. However, it begins by examining two variables (social class and race) that are not correlated with autism then discusses those that are associated with autism (gender, mental retardation, genetic disorders, neurological disorders, and other disabilities).

Social class. Kanner's (1943) initial report suggested that autism tended to affect children from homes with higher levels of education and SES status. However, current research has not confirmed this trend and it is now concluded that autism affects all SES levels. Explanations for the prior findings include that those in the lower SES groups previously lacked access to the services that would result in an autism diagnosis (Tidmarsh & Volkmar, 2003).

Race. Yeargin-Allsopp and colleagues (2003) have documented that rates of autism are "remarkably similar when examined by race" (p. 51). Interestingly, however, among the population of preschoolers (ages 3 to 5 years) who qualify for *IDEA* special education services, more "White (not Hispanic)" children are more likely to be classified as autistic (14,405) then they are to be classified mentally retarded (13,385). Conversely, "Black (not Hispanic)" and "Hispanic" preschoolers are more likely to be classified as mentally retarded (4,038 and 4,128 respectively) than autistic (2,283 and 3,732 respectively; US Department of Education, 2003). Given the similar rates of autism found across racial groups, these data are surprising and disturbing. It may be that there is a greater willingness to diagnosis minority children as retarded and conversely a greater reluctance to classify white children as such.

Gender. Especially among individuals with high-functioning autism (Tidmarsh & Volkmar, 2003), it is clear that more males than females are diagnosed with autism (Centers for Disease Control and Prevention, 1998; Kielinen, Linna, & Moilanen, 2000). Yeargin-Allsopp and colleagues (2003) report that as the severity of mental retardation increases, the gender ratio decreases (from 4.4:1 to 1.3:1). In addition, Yeargin-Allsopp and colleagues report that the predominance of males is consistent across ethnic groups (i.e., 3.8:1 among whites, 4.3:1 among blacks, and 3.5:1 within other racial groups). Fombonne's (2003b) review of the epidemiology of autism suggested the male to female ratio of autism to vary considerably (from 1.33:1 to 16.0:1), with an average 4.8:1. Unfortunately, it appears that the high frequency of males with autism has been given relatively little research attention (Tidmarsh & Volkmar, 2003).

Mental retardation. With the exception of those diagnosed with Asperger's Disorder, the *DSM IV-TR* (APA, 2000) suggests that a majority of children with autism will have mental retardation (*DSM* does not address cognitive functioning in its discussion of PDD-NOS). However, in a recent study of 15,500 preschool-aged children in England, it was reported that among those identified with autism ($n = 97$) only 26 percent were mentally retarded. In addition it was found that patterns of cognitive functioning varied significantly according to the type of autism spectrum disorder diagnosed. Specifically, 30.8 percent of children with Autistic Disorder, 92.4 percent with PDD-NOS, and 100 percent of children with Asperger's Disorder had measured intelligence in the normal range. Of those children with Autistic Disorder who were mentally retarded, 50 percent had measured IQs in the mild to moderate deficit range, and 19.2 percent had IQ scores in the severe to profound deficit range (Chakrabarti & Fombonne, 2001). Combined with the results of other recent surveys (Centers for Disease Control, 1998; Kielinen et al., 2000), Chakrabarti and Fombonne suggest that as a group, children with autism are "... less impaired than what has been classically described" (p. 3097) and that "there appears to be a downward trend for the rate of mental retardation within the group narrowly defined as autism" (pp. 3097–3098). These researchers suggest that this finding may be an indication that the very early and intensive intervention that is now offered to children with autism is associated with improved cognitive functioning outcomes.

Whereas most research has examined the rate of mental retardation among children with autism, Nordin and Gillberg (1996) examined the prevalence of autism in the population of Swedish children with mental retardation. The authors used a rigorous diagnostic system to identify children with three subgroups of autism spectrum disorder: Autistic Disorder (those who met 8 of the *DSM III-R* criteria), autistic-like condition (those who met 6 of the *DSM III-R* criteria), and autism spectrum disorder not otherwise specified (those who had autistic symptomatology but did not present symptoms with enough severity for the *DSM III-R* classification). The study procedures entailed an initial period of screening in 1991 and a follow-up screening in 1993. The results indicate that autistic disorder is present in 8.9 percent of mentally retarded children. In addition, they found that it is more prevalent among children with severe mental retardation than among those with mild to moderate mental retardation.

Genetic disorders. In 1996, Kielinen, Rantala, Timonen, Linna, and Moilanen (2004) conducted a population-based survey of 152,732 children and adolescents less than 16 years of age who lived in northern Finland. Of the 187 identified as children with autism, 12.3 percent had a known or suspected genetic disorder, the most common of which were Down Syndrome (3.7 percent) and fragile X syndrome (2.1 percent). In a recent review article, Muhle, Trentacoste, and Rapin (2004) report rates of tuberous sclerosis among individuals with autism to range from 1.1 to 1.3 percent.

Neurological disorders. As was mentioned in Chapter 1, one of the first indications that autism was a brain-based disorder (and not due to inadequate parenting) was its association with epilepsy. Recent research confirms that this disorder continues to be the most common neurological condition found among children with autism. It has been observed in 18.2 percent of children with autism (Kielinen et al., 2004). Level of cognitive functioning is an important correlate of seizure activity among children with autism. Whereas it is particularly high among children with low measured intelligence, it is relatively low among those with normal or only mild cognitive deficits. Thus, school professionals should be especially attentive for signs of seizure activity among students with low-functioning autism. The risk of seizures appears especially high among children with Rett's and Childhood Disintegrative Disorders (Tidmarsh & Volkmar, 2003). Other neurological disorders identified by Kielinen and colleagues (2004) include cerebral palsy (4.3 percent) and a variety of other conditions (e.g., hydrocephalus, 3.2 percent; neonatal meningitis/encephalitis, 2.7 percent; and fetal alcohol syndrome, 1.1 percent).

Other disabilities. Additional disorders suggested by Kielinen and colleagues (2004) to be common among children with autism include vision impairment (23 percent) and hearing impairment (8.6 percent).

Concluding Comments Regarding the Incidence of Autism

Epidemiological studies are useful in establishing a baseline regarding the prevalence of the disorder and have served to refine the criteria for diagnosing autism and differentiating it from disorders with similar symptomatology. Epidemiological research has also done much to further our knowledge regarding the possible etiologic role of genetic factors and medical disorders. The heterogeneity of the population of children with autistic disorder revealed in epidemiological data suggests that there are a host of risk factors implicated in the development of autism. In addition, current epidemiological research suggests a significant increase in the prevalence of autism. Reasons for this increase include a real increase in the number of children with this disorder, and artificially induced changes such as a loosening of diagnostic criteria and/or increased awareness of autism and autism spectrum disorders. Future epidemiological research will continue to enhance our understanding of the prevalence of autism extended to include the entire spectrum of the disorder and the contribution of potential risk factors.

4
Case Finding and Screening

From the findings mentioned in Chapters 1 and 3, it is clear that school professionals must be vigilant for the symptoms of autism among the students they serve. All school professionals need to be willing and able to engage in case finding, and school psychologists and special education personnel also need to be able to screen for autism and make appropriate referrals for diagnostic assessments. Although it is anticipated that not all school psychologists will have had the supervised training experiences required to be able to diagnose a specific autism spectrum disorder, it is expected that all school psychologists will know how to assist in the process of diagnosing these disorders. In addition, all school psychologists should be able to conduct psychoeducational assessments of students with autism to determine learning strengths and challenges, as well as to help determine special education eligibility and develop IEP goals and objectives (Shriver, Allen, & Mathews, 1999). Relationships among these identification steps are summarized in Figure 4.1, which presents an adaptation of Filipek and her colleague's (1999) algorithm for the process of diagnosing autism. This chapter examines the first two elements of the identification process: case finding and screening. Chapters 5 and 6 discuss the latter two elements: diagnostic and psychoeducational assessments.

Case Finding

Case finding refers to routine developmental surveillance of all students in the general population to identify atypical developmental patterns. Case finding efforts do not diagnose autism or other developmental disorders; rather they are designed to recognize the presence of risk factors and/or warning signs and the need for further screening and evaluation. Ideally provided by primary care providers at well-baby check-ups, school personnel involved in infant and preschool programs also play an important role in case finding (as mandated by Child Find regulations). Given the fact that not all instances of autism will be identified before children enter school, *all school professionals should be expected to engage in case finding*. For school psychologists and special education personnel, this would include training general educators to identify the risk factors for and warning signs of autism.

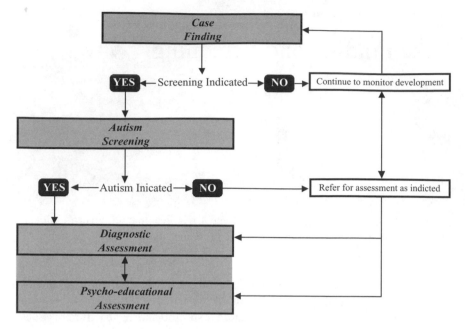

FIGURE 4.1. Adaptation of Filipek et al.'s (1999) Algorithm for the Process of Diagnosing Autism. *Note*: Adapted with kind permission of Springer Science and Business Media. Copyright © 1999 Plenum Publishing Corporation.

Case finding involves *looking, listening*, and *questioning*. First, school professionals need to look for and be able to recognize autism risk factors and warning signs. Such "looking" may include school-wide developmental screening and staff development. Second, school professionals (especially school psychologists) need to be good listeners and able to recognize caregiver concerns that signal the possible presence of autism symptoms. Finally, they need to know how to question caregivers so as to further identify autism symptoms.

Looking

Risk factors. According to Newschaffer, Fallin, and Lee (2002): "The only identifiable group known for certain to have a substantively elevated ASD risk is siblings of affected individuals" (p. 139). Thus, special attention needs to be directed toward the siblings of individuals diagnosed with autism. Those who display any symptom of autism should be immediately screened for these disorders. Other risk factors that might be classified as having some association with ADS and can be considered moderate risk factors include a prior diagnosis of tuberous sclerosis, fragile X syndrome, or epilepsy, and/or the presence of a family history of autism or autistic-like behaviors (Filipek et al., 1999, 2000).

TABLE 4.1. Warning signs of autism.

- No big smiles or other joyful expressions by 6 months.[b]
- No back-and-forth sharing of sounds, smiles, or facial expressions by 9 months.[b]
- No back-and-forth gestures, such as pointing, showing, reaching or waving bye-bye by 12 months.[a,b]
- No babbling at 12 months.[a,b]
- No single words at 16 months.[a,b]
- No 2-word spontaneous (nonecholalic) phrases by 24 months.[a,b]
- Failure to attend to human voice by 24 months.[c]
- Failure to look at face and eyes of others by 24 months.[c]
- Failure to orient to name by 24 months.[c]
- Failure to demonstrate interest in other children by 24 months.[c]
- Failure to imitate by 24 months.[c]
- Any loss of any language or social skill at any age.[a,b]

Note: Sources [a]Filipek et al., 1999; [b]Greenspan, 1999; and [c]Ozonoff, 2003.

Currently, there is no substantive evidence supporting any one non-genetic risk factor for autism. However, given that there are likely different causes of autism, it is possible that yet to be identified non-heritable risk factors may prove to be important in certain subgroups of individuals with this disorder. Hence, there may be an interaction between the presence of specific genetic defects and specific environmental factors. As was discussed in Chapter 2, individuals with a particular genetic predisposition for autism may have a greater risk of developing this disorder subsequent to exposure to certain non-genetic risk factors. In particular, it has been suggested that obstetric suboptimality; prenatal maternal infection (e.g., rubella, cytomegalovirus, herpes, HIV) and drug exposure (e.g., thalidomide, valproic acid, alcohol abuse); and postnatal infections (e.g., herpes encephalitis) and viruses (e.g., chicken pox) are associated with an increased risk for autism (Hansen & Hagerman, 2003; Newschaffer et al., 2002).

Warning signs. Whereas the presence of risk factors signals the need to be vigilant for symptoms of autism, observation of warning signs provides concrete evidence suggestive of these disorders. From several different sources (Filipek et al., 2000; Greenspan, 1999; Ozonoff, 2003), Table 4.1 provides a list of warning signs that are considered *absolute indicators* of the need for an autism screening.

When looking for warning signs, it is imperative to keep in mind that the symptoms of autism will vary according to developmental level. Specifically, during infancy warning signs may include not being comforted by (or interested in) being held and limited social smiling, eye contact, vocalization, and social play. In early childhood, warning signs may include preferring to be alone, not showing any emotion upon separation from or reunification with parents, becoming very upset with changes in routine or environment, echolalic speech, odd repetitive motor behavior, and unusual attachments to objects. As a child progresses through childhood, failure to make friends or display social/emotional reciprocity are considered warning signs. In middle childhood, warning signs include rarely sharing interests with others, and limited social and verbal expression and social interactions.

Finally, in adolescence warning signs of autism include having few if any friends and failing to understand social rules and conventions. Unusual affect, persistent and repetitive speech and/or behaviors are also considered warning signs (Jelline, Patel, & Froehle, 2002).

Developmental screening. In addition to being able to recognize and respond to the warning signs described above, case finding may also include more proactive strategies such as school-based developmental screenings. These activities would help not only to identify developmental variations that are consistent with autism, but will also help to identify other developmental disorders. As such, these screenings would be consistent with the federal regulations known as "child find." A component of the *Individuals with Disabilities Education Improvement Act* (IDEIA), child find regulations require school professionals to identify, locate, and evaluate all children with disabilities, aged birth to 21, who are in need of early intervention or special education services (see http://www.childfindidea.org/overview.htm for more information about these regulations). *IDEIA* 2004'*s* greater emphasis on early identification and screening would appear to strengthen and further enable Child Find mandates (Klotz & Nealis, 2005).

Developmental screening techniques suggested by Filipek and colleagues (1999) as having "acceptable psychometric properties" (p. 451) include *The Ages and Stages Questionnaire* (Bricker & Squires, 1994); *The BIRGANCE® Screens* (Birgance, 1986); *The Child Development Inventories* (Ireton, 1992); and *The Parents' Evaluation of Developmental Status* (Glascoe, 1997). Recently, Brereton, Tonge, MacKinnon, and Einfeld (2002) reported that the *Developmental Behavior Checklist* (Einfeld & Tonge, 1995) is also an effective autism screening instrument for individuals ages 4 to 17 years of age.

Staff development. Efforts to educate teachers about the risk factors and warning signs of autism would also be consistent with child find regulations, and the recent *IDEIA* reauthorization appears to increase the availability of federal funding for such training (Klotz & Nealis, 2005). Giving general and special education teachers the information they need to look for autism (such as is presented in this section) will facilitate case finding efforts.

Listening

When parents have concerns about their child's development, they are usually correct (Filipek et al., 1999; Galscoe, 1997). Especially in light of reports that parents of children with autism typically have concerns about their children by 18 to 19 months of age (De Giacomo & Fombonne, 1998; Rogers, 2001), it is critical for school professionals to listen, REALLY LISTEN, to parents when they express such concerns. Table 4.2 provides the Filipek and colleagues (1999) list of parental concerns that are considered "red flags" for autism. The greater the number of these concerns expressed, the greater the need for an immediate autism screening. Whereas isolated communication concerns may be indicative of expressive language delays (and not necessarily autism), social concerns (especially

TABLE 4.2. Filipek et al.'s (1999, p. 452) list of parental concerns that are "red flags" for autism.

Social concerns	Communication concerns	Behavioral concerns
• Does not smile socially • Seems to prefer to play alone • Is very independent • Has poor eye contact • Is in his/her own world • Tunes us out • Is not interested in other children	• Does not respond to his/her name • Cannot tell me what s/he wants • Does not follow directions • Appears deaf at times • Seems to hear sometimes but not others • Does not point or wave bye-bye	• Tantrums • Is hyperactive/uncooperative or oppositional • Doesn't know how to play with toys • Does the same thing over and over • Toe walks • Has unusual attachments to toys (e.g., always holding a certain object) • Lines things up • Is oversensitive to certain textures or sounds • Has odd finger and/or body movement patterns

Note: Reprinted with kind permission of Springer Science and Business Media. Copyright © 1999 Plenum Publishing Corporation.

when combined with co-existing communication and behavioral concerns) are particularly important red flags of autism (Filipek et al., 1999).

Questioning

Although parental concerns about atypical development are powerful indicators of the need for screenings, the absence of such does not necessarily eliminate the possibility of autism. Further, as was mentioned above, isolated communication concerns may be indicative of expressive language delays (not autism), and consequently it will be important for those engaged in case finding efforts to be prepared to ask questions about social and behavioral concerns. Thus, it is critical for school professionals to be able to ask questions that will facilitate the identification of behaviors consistent with autism. Filipek and colleagues' (1999) list of such questions is provided in Table 4.3.

Screening

All students at risk for autism (as identified by case finding efforts) should be screened for this disorder. Such screening is designed to help determine the need for additional diagnostic assessments. Because these screenings are relatively quick and easy, it has been suggested that screening referral decisions should be rather liberal. According to Filipek and colleagues (1999, 2000), autism screenings should include lead screening, audiological evaluations, and behavioral screenings. *All school psychologists should be prepared to participate in the behavioral screening*

TABLE 4.3. Adaptation of Filipek et al.'s (1999, p. 453) autism behavior identification questions.

Socialization ("Does she/he ...")
- cuddle like other children?
- look at you when you are talking or playing?
- smile in response to a smile from others?
- engage in reciprocal, back-and-forth play?
- play simple imitation games, such as pat-a-cake or peek-a-boo?
- show interest in other children?

Communication ("Does she/he ...")
- point with his/her finger?
- gesture? Nod yes and no?
- direct your attention by holding up objects for you to see?
- have odd speech?
- show things to people?
- lead an adult by the hand?
- give inconsistent response to his/her name? ... to commands?
- use rote, repetitive, or echolalic speech?
- memorize strings of words or scripts?

Behavior ("Does she/he ...")
- have repetitive, stereotyped, or odd motor behavior?
- have preoccupations or a narrow range of interests?
- attend more to parts of objects (e.g., the wheels of a toy car)?
- have limited or absent pretend play?
- imitate other people's actions?
- play with toys in the same exact way each time?
- appear strongly attached to a specific unusual object(s)?

Note: Adapted with kind permission of Springer Science and Business Media. Copyright © 1999 Plenum Publishing.

of the student who has risk factors and/or displays warning signs of autism. It is important to reiterate that the purpose of screening is not to diagnose autism, but rather to determine if such diagnostic assessments are warranted. *All school psychologists should be able to distinguish between screening and diagnosis.*

Lead Screening

From research suggesting that individuals with autism have higher blood lead concentrations, and the hypothesis that lead poisoning may contribute to the onset or acceleration of the development of the symptoms of autism, lead screening is recommended for all children referred for an autism screening (Deisinger, 2001). Such testing would be especially critical if there are reports of the student displaying pica and/or those who live in environments with an increased risk for lead exposure (Filipek et al., 1999; 2000). Although school professionals are not expected to conduct this type of testing, it is important for them to know about the lead screening's role in screening for autism.

Audiological Assessment

The hearing tests conducted as part of any autism screening must be comprehensive in nature. Typically, the standard school hearing screening is not sufficient. To the extent that hearing loss explains autistic-like behaviors, referrals to the appropriate audiologist, speech-language pathologist, and/or medical practioner should be made. However, to the extent that there are other warning signs of autism that are not explained by a hearing loss (i.e., social and behavioral concerns), additional screening and evaluation should take place. In addition, it is important to keep in mind that autism can co-occur with hearing loss. Thus, although a hearing loss would argue against the need for additional autism diagnostic evaluations, school professionals working with these students should continue to be vigilant for indicators of autism and make additional diagnostic referrals as indicated (Filipek et al., 1999; 2000). Here again, most school professionals are not expected to conduct this type of testing. However, it is important for them to know about the importance of an audiological assessment in screening for autism.

Behavioral Screening

Given their training in behavioral observation and knowledge of the appropriate use of behavior rating scales, school psychologists are exceptionally well qualified to conduct the behavioral screening of students suspected to have autism. Several screening tools are available to assist in this process. Initially, most of these available screening tools focused on the identification of autism among infants and preschool-age children. More recently, however, screening tools useful for the identification of school-aged children who have high-functioning autism or Asperger's Disorder have been developed.

Screening tools for infants and preschoolers. One of the first tools to show promise in the very early screening for autism is the *CHecklist for Autism in Toddlers* (CHAT; Baird et al., 2000; Baron-Cohen, Allen, & Gillberg, 1992; Baron-Cohen et al., 1996; Baron-Cohen et al., 2000; Scambler, Rogers, & Wehner, 2001). Designed to identify risk of autism among 18-month-old children, the *CHAT* takes 5 to 10 minutes to administer and would be useful to the school psychologist working in infant and preschool programs. It is the most widely researched of the screening instruments (Goin & Myers, 2004). A sample of this screening tool is provided in Table 4.4. The *CHAT* consists of nine questions asked of the parent (Section A), and five items completed by the screener that require direct observation of the child (Section B). Of the 14 *CHAT* items, 5 are considered to be "key items" (Items A5, A7, Bii, Biii, Biv in Table 4.5). These key items, which assess joint attention and pretend play, have been found to be powerful predictors of the diagnosis of Autistic Disorder. If a student fails all five of these items, they are considered to be at high risk for autism. If a student fails items A7 and Biv, they are considered to have a medium risk for developing this disorder. A re-screening one month after the first is recommended for all children who fail the CHAT, and any child who fails it for

TABLE 4.4. *Checklist of Autism in Toddlers* (CHAT; Baron-Cohen et al., 1992, p. 842).

SECTION A: History: Ask parent . . .

1. Does your child enjoy being swung, bounced on your knee, etc.?	YES	NO
2. Does your child take an interest in other children?	YES	NO
3. Does your child like climbing on things, such as up stairs?	YES	NO
4. Does your child enjoy playing peek-a-boo/hide-and-seek?	YES	NO
5. Does your child ever PRETEND, for example to make a cup of tea using a toy cup and teapot, or pretend other things?	YES	NO
6. Does your child ever use his/her index finger to point to ASK for something?	YES	NO
7. Does your child ever use his/her index finger to point to indicate INTEREST in something?	YES	NO
8. Can your child play properly with small toys (e.g., cars or bricks) without just mouthing, fiddling or dropping them?	YES	NO
9. Does your child ever bring objects over to you (parent) to SHOW you something?	YES	NO

Section B: general practitioner or health visitor observation

i. During the appointment, has the child made eye contact with you?	YES	NO
ii. Get child's attention, then point across the room at an interesting object and say *'Oh look! There's a [name of toy!]'*. Watch child's face. Does the child look across to see what you are pointing at?	YES	NO*
iii. Get the child's attention, then give child a miniature toy cup and teapot and say *'Can you make a cup of tea?'* Does the child pretend to pour out tea, drink it, etc.?	YES	NO†
iv. Say to the child *'Where is the light?,'* or *'Show me the light'*. Does the child POINT with his/her index finger at the light?	YES	NO‡
v. Can the child build a tower of bricks? (if so how many?) (No. of bricks ____)	YES	NO

   * To record Yes on this item, ensure the child has not simply looked at your hand, but has actually looked at the object you are pointing at.

   † If you can elicit an example of pretending in some other game, score a Yes on this item.

   ‡ Repeat this with *'Where's the teddy?'* or some other unreachable object, if child does not understand the word light. To record YES on this item, the child must have looked up at your face around the time of pointing.

Scoring: ☐ High risk for autism: Fails A5, A7, Bii, Biii, and Biv
         ☐ Medium risk for autism: Fails A7, Biv (but not in maximum risk group)
         ☐ Low risk for autism (not in other two risk groups)

Note: Reprinted with permission from the British Journal of Psychiatry. Copyright © 1992, The Royal College of Physicians.

a second time should be referred for a diagnostic assessment (Baron-Cohen et al., 2000; Wheelwright, 1995). The other *CHAT* items provide additional information designed to allow the screener to differentiate an autistic-like profile from that of a student with a more global developmental delay.

Support for the use of this screening tool comes from research suggesting that 83 percent of 18-month-old children within one sample ($n = 16,000$), who failed the five key items administered twice one month apart, were subsequently diagnosed with autistic disorder at 42 months of age. Conversely, none of the children in the low-risk group could be assigned this diagnosis at 42 months (Baron-Cohen et al., 1996). Although the *CHAT* appears to have promise for the identification

TABLE 4.5. *Modified Checklist for Autism in Toddlers* (M-CHAT; Robins et al., 2001, p. 142).

Please fill out the following about how your child *usually* is. Please try to answer every question. If the behavior is rare (e.g., you've seen it once or twice), please answer as if the child does not do it.

1. Does your child enjoy being swung, bounced on your knee, etc.?	Yes	No
2. Does your child take an interest in other children?	Yes	No
3. Does your child like climbing on things, such as up stairs?	Yes	No
4. Does your child enjoy playing peek-a-boo/hide-and-seek?	Yes	No
5. Does your child ever pretend, for example, to talk on the phone or take care of dolls, or pretend other things?	Yes	No
6. Does your child ever use his/her index finger to point, to ask for something?	Yes	No
7. Does your child ever use his/her index finger to point, to indicate interest in something?	Yes	No
8. Can your child play properly with small toys (e.g., cars or bricks) without just mouthing, fiddling, or dropping them?	Yes	No
9. Does your child ever bring objects over to you (parent) to show you something?	Yes	No
10. Does your child look you in the eye for more than a second or two?	Yes	No
11. Does your child ever seem oversensitive to noise? (e.g., plugging ears)	Yes	No
12. Does your child smile in response to your face or your smile?	Yes	No
13. Does your child imitate you? (e.g., if you make a face—will your child imitate it?)	Yes	No
14. Does your child respond to his/her name when you call?	Yes	No
15. If you point at a toy across the room, does your child look at it?	Yes	No
16. Does your child walk?	Yes	No
17. Does your child look at things you are looking at?	Yes	No
18. Does your child make unusual finger movements near his/her face?	Yes	No
19. Does your child try to attract your attention to his/her own activity?	Yes	No
20. Have you ever wondered if your child is deaf?	Yes	No
21. Does your child understand what people say?	Yes	No
22. Does your child sometimes stare at nothing or wander with no purpose?	Yes	No
23. Does your child look at your face to check your reaction when faced with something unfamiliar?	Yes	No

M-CHAT Scoring Instructions

A child fails the checklist when 2 or more critical items are failed OR when any three items are failed. Yes/no answers convert to pass/fail responses. Below are listed the failed responses for each item on the M-CHAT. Bold capitalized items are CRITICAL items. Not all children who fail the checklist will meet criteria for a diagnosis on the autism spectrum. However, children who fail the checklist should be evaluated in more depth by the physician or referred for a developmental evaluation with a specialist.

1. No	6. No	11. Yes	16. No	21. No
2. NO	**7. NO**	12. No	17. No	22. Yes
3. No	8. No	**13. NO**	18. Yes	23. No
4. No	**9. NO**	**14. NO**	19. No	
5. No	10. No	**15. NO**	20. Yes	

of Autistic Disorder among a subset of very young children (i.e., those with more severe symptoms of this disorder), it is important to note that this measure is less sensitive to the less severe symptoms of autism (Kabot, Masi, & Segal, 2003).

Children with milder symptoms of autism, such as those displayed by children who were later diagnosed with Asperger's Disorder or high-functioning autism, did not routinely fail the *CHAT* at 18 months. A six-year follow-up of a community sample of 16,235 children screened with the 2-stage *CHAT* found that higher functioning children (those with higher IQs) were missed by this screening (Baird et al., 2000). At the same time, however, this study revealed an extremely low false positive rate. In other words, children who fail the *CHAT* will likely go on to later be diagnosed with autism. Specifically, for the broader autism spectrum, the 2-stage *CHAT* had a positive predictive value [true positives/(true positives + false positives)] of 59 percent, a sensitivity [true positives/(true positives + false negatives)] of 21 percent, and a specificity [true negatives/(true negatives + false positives)] of 99.9 percent.

Another screening tool for use with very young children, the *Modified Checklist of Autism in Toddlers* (M-CHAT; Robins, Fein, Barton, & Green, 2001), is purported to be more sensitive to the broader autism spectrum. Using the 9 items from the original *CHAT* as its basis, the 23-item *M-CHAT* is designed to screen for autism at 24 months of age. A sample of the *M-CHAT* is provided in Table 4.5. Unlike the *CHAT*, the *M-CHAT* does not require the screener to directly observe the child. This questionnaire makes use of a "Yes/No" format and can be completed by a caregiver before a screening appointment. Answers are converted to pass/fail responses by the screener and a child fails the checklist when two or more of six critical items are failed or when any three items are failed. Among 1,293 10- to 30-month-old children screened for autism with the *M-CHAT*, 58 were referred for a diagnostic/developmental evaluation. Of these 58, 39 (67 percent) were subsequently diagnosed with an autism spectrum disorder. Preliminary psychometric data suggests that when a positive autism screen is based upon failure of two of the six critical items, the *M-CHAT* has a sensitivity (the proportion of children with autism who have a screening test result suggestive of autism) of 95 percent, specificity (the proportion of children without autism who have a screening test result suggesting they are free of these disorders) of 99 percent, positive predictive power (the percentage of children who have a screening test result suggestive of autism who actually do have one of these disorders) of 79 percent, and negative predictive power (the percentage of children who have a screening test result suggesting they are free of these disorders who actually do not have autism) of 99 percent. Using the criteria of any three items failed, the *M-CHAT's* sensitivity was 97 percent, specificity was 95 percent, and positive predictive value was 36 percent (Robins et al., 2001).

Wong and colleagues (2004) combined elements of the *CHAT* (developed in the United Kingdom) and *M-CHAT* (developed in the United States) to create a screening tool for Chinese children with autism in Hong Kong. Referred to as the *CHAT-23*, this screening tool combines the 23 questions of the *M-CHAT* (Section A) and the observation section (Section B) of the original *CHAT* in a two-stage screening process. An English translation of this measure is provided in Table 4.6.

The first stage of this screening involves the use of the 23 questions of the *M-CHAT*. However, in the *CHAT-23* the "Yes/No" format of the *M-CHAT* is replaced with a graded response format (i.e., never, seldom, usually, often) after it was found that the parents in this sample of Chinese children found it difficult to give definite answers to simple yes/no questions (with question 16 maintaining the yes/no response format). Answering "seldom" or "never" to any two of seven key questions (Items 2, 5, 7, 9, 13, 15, and 23) or any six of all 23 questions was defined as positive for autism on Part A. For Part B, failure (which means the test is positive for autism) was defined as not passing at least two of the first four items.

To study the efficacy of this screening tool, 276 13- to 86-month-old children were recruited by Wong and colleagues (2004) for a study. The final sample including 87 children with autism or PDD (group 1) and 68 normally developing children and 80 children with developmental delays other than autism (group 2). Analysis of Part A results revealed that failing two or more of the seven key items correctly identified 93 percent of the children with autism (group 1), and failing any 6 of all 23 identified 84 percent of the children in this group. The number of false positives was low with the specificity scores of these two failure criteria being 77 and 85 percent, respectively. The positive predictive value of these two criteria was high, falling at 70 and 80 percent, respectively. On Part B, failing any two of the first four items correctly identified 74 percent, and corresponded to a specificity of 92 percent and a positive predictive value of 85 percent. Wong and colleagues (2004) suggest that this measure could be used as a two-stage screening with Part A's questionnaire serving as the first stage, and the Part B's behavior observations (conducted by a trained child care professional) serving as a second step for those children who scored positive for autism on the questionnaire.

A final screening tool designed for very young children (ages 12 to 48 months) and developed for use within both general and clinical populations is the *Pervasive Developmental Disorders Screening Test—II* (PDDST-II; Siegel, 2004). Published by PsychCorp, this measure has three stages, with the *PDDST-II: Stage 1* designed to help determine if a given child should be evaluated for autism and is the one that the school psychologist working in general education settings would find helpful. *Stage 2* is intended for use within a developmental clinic and is designed to discriminate between children with autism and those who have other related developmental disorders such as language delays and mental retardation. *Stage 3* is intended for use within an autism specialty clinic and is designed to discriminate children with Autistic Disorder from other autism spectrum disorders. Each of these rating scales is designed to be completed by parents and should take no more than 15 minutes to complete and 5 minutes to score.

TABLE 4.6. English version of the *CHAT-23* (Wong et al., 2004, p. 176).

Section A: Self-Administered Questionnaire
Please fill out the following about how your child usually is. This questionnaire should be administered by the chief caregiver of the child. Please fill the corresponding circle black completely.

	Never	Rarely	Sometimes	Often
1. Does your child enjoy being swung, bounced on your knee, etc.?	○	○	○	○
2. Does your child take an interest in other children?	○	○	○	○
3. Does your child like climbing on things, such as up stairs?	○	○	○	○
4. Does your child enjoy playing peek-a-boo/hide-and-seek?	○	○	○	○
5. Does your child ever pretend, for example, to talk on the phone or take care of dolls, or pretend other things?	○	○	○	○
6. Does your child ever use his/her index finger to point, to ask for something?	○	○	○	○
7. Does your child ever use his/her index finger to point, to indicate interest in something?	○	○	○	○
8. Can your child play properly with small toys (e.g., cars or bricks) without just mouthing, fiddling, or dropping them?	○	○	○	○
9. Does your child ever bring objects over to you (parent) to show you something?	○	○	○	○
10. Does your child look you in the eye for more than a second or two?	○	○	○	○
11. Does your child ever seem oversensitive to noise? (e.g., plugging ears)	○	○	○	○
12. Does your child smile in response to your face or your smile?	○	○	○	○
13. Does your child imitate you? (e.g., if you make a face—will your child imitate it?)	○	○	○	○
14. Does your child respond to his/her name when you call?	○	○	○	○
15. If you point at a toy across the room, does your child look at it?	○	○	○	○
16. Does your child walk?	Yes ⇨	○	○	⇦ No
17. Does your child look at things you are looking at?	○	○	○	○
18. Does your child make unusual finger movements near his/her face?	○	○	○	○
19. Does your child try to attract your attention to his/her own activity?	○	○	○	○
20. Have you ever wondered if your child is deaf?	○	○	○	○
21. Does your child understand what people say?	○	○	○	○
22. Does your child sometimes stare at nothing or wander with no purpose?	○	○	○	○
23. Does your child look at your face to check your reaction when faced with something unfamiliar?	○	○	○	○

TABLE 4.6. *Continued*

Section B: Interview (for investigator use only)				
1. During the appointment, has the child made eye contact with you?	Never ◯	Rarely ◯	Sometimes ◯	Often ◯
2. Get child's attention, then point across the room at an interesting object and say *'Oh look! There's a [name of toy]'*. Watch child's face. Does the child look across to see what you are pointing at?			Yes ◯	No ◯
3. Get the child's attention, then give child a miniature toy cup and teapot and say *'Can you make a cup of tea?'* Does the child pretend to pour out tea, drink it, etc.?		Yes ◯	Imitate ◯	Never ◯
4. Say to the child *'Where is the light?'*, or *'Show me the light'*. Does the child POINT with his/her index finger at the light?	Never ◯	Point only ◯	Look Only ◯	Point & Look ◯
5. Can the child build a tower of bricks? (if so how many?) (No. of bricks ____)			Yes ◯	No ◯

Item 5 is for testing the general developmental age. United Kingdom: Original CHAT Part A (questions 1–9) and part B; discriminant questions/items are A5, A7, B3, and B4; United States, Part A (questions 1–23) only; discriminant questions are 2, 7, 9, 13, 14, and 15 (any 2 or 6 questions or any 3 of 23 questions; Hong Kong Chinese: CHAT-23, part A (questions 1–23) and part B, discriminant questions/items are 2, 5, 7, 9, 13, 15, and 23 (any 2 of 7 questions or any 6 or 23). Only question 7 is most discriminative and appears in all 3 CHAT forms as a screening tool for autism.

Note: Reproduced with permission from *Pediatrics*, Vol. 114 (2), Pages e166–e176, Copyright © 2004 by the AAP.

If five or more of the *Stage 1* items are checked as being "YES, Usually True," then the result is considered a positive finding, and a diagnostic evaluation for possible autism (as well as some other developmental disorders) is indicated. The *PDDST-II* manual also includes a 41-item reproducible supplemental questionnaire that can be used to gain additional information from parents and is suggested to be helpful in identifying other disorders related to autism that may require additional assessment.

Psychometric data was obtained by studying the *PDDST-II: Stage 1's* ability to delineate 681 children referred for autism assessment from 256 children who were part of a study of very low birth weight pre-term infants. Results of this study suggested that the *PDDST-II: Stage 1* has a sensitivity of .92 percent, and specificity of .91 percent (Siegel, 2004). The psychometric data for this and other infant and preschool autism screening tests is provided in Table 4.7.

Screening tools for school-age children. Developed by Ehlers and Gillberg (1993), *The High Functioning Autism Spectrum Screening Questionnaire (ASSQ)* is a checklist designed to be completed by parents and/or teachers. A sample of this questionnaire is provided in Table 4.8. The 27 *ASSQ* items are rated on a 3-point scale (with 0 indicating normality, 1 some abnormality, and 2 definite abnormality) and has a total score range from 0 to 54. Questionnaire content includes 11 social

TABLE 4.7. Infant and preschooler autism screening measures: Sensitivity (Sen.) and specificity (Spe.).

Measure	Sample	Sen.	Spe.
CHAT: Stage 1[a]	16,235 general population 18-month-olds (*Note:* This is the only general population sample)	.35	.98
CHAT: Stage 2[a]	60 19-month-olds. All 38 identified by Stage 1 as high risk, and 22 of 188 identified as medium risk	.21	.99
M-CHAT: 2/6[b]	1122 18- to 25-month-old well-baby checkups, and 171 18- to 30-month old early intervention recipients (using 2 of 6 critical items criteria)	.95	.99
M-CHAT: 3/23[b]	1122 18- to 25-month-old well-baby checkups, and 171 18- to 30-month old early intervention recipients (using 3 of all 23 items criteria)	.97	.95
CHAT-23: Pt A, 2/7[c]	87 children with autism vs. 68 normal & 80 developmentally delayed 13- to 86-month-olds (using Part A, 2 of 7 critical items criteria)	.93	.77
CHAT-23: Pt A, 6/23[c]	87 children with autism vs. 68 normal & 80 developmentally delayed 13- to 86-month-olds (using Part A, 6 of all 23 items criteria)	.84	.85
CHAT-23: Pt B[c]	87 children with autism vs. 68 normal & 80 developmentally delayed 13- to 86-month-olds (using Part B)	.74	.92
PDDST-II: Stage 1[d]	681 autism referrals vs. 256 very low birth weight pre-term 12- to 14-month olds	.92	.91
PDDST-II: Stage 2[d]	490 children with autism vs. 194 with other neuropsychiatric disorders (not autistic)	.73	.49

Sources: [a]Baird et al. (2002), [b]Robins et al. (2001), [c]Wong et al. (2004), [d]Siegel (2004).
Note: Sensitivity indicates the probability that a child with autism will test positive (be suggested to have autism). Specificity indicates the probability that a child without autism will test negative (be suggested not to have autism).

interaction items, 6 communication items, 5 restricted/repetitive behavior items, and 5 motor clumsiness and other associated symptom items.

The initial epidemiological study that employed this questionnaire included 1,401 7- to 16-year-olds. The mean score for this sample was 0.7 (*SD*, 2.6). Among the five participants who were "definite Asperger syndrome cases" (p. 139), the mean score was 26.2 (*SD*, 10.3). A subsequent validation study with a smaller clinical group (*n* = 110) suggested this measure to be "a reliable and valid parent and teacher screening instrument of high-functioning autism spectrum disorders in a clinical setting" (Ehlers, Gillberg, & Wing, 1999, p. 139).

From data provided by Ehlers et al. (1999), two separate sets of cutoff scores are suggested. The first set of scores (parents, 13 and teachers, 11) is suggested to be indicative of "socially impaired children" (p. 139), but not necessarily those with autism. Although minimizing the risk of false negatives (especially for milder cases of autism), this set of scores is associated with a high rate of false positives (23 percent for parents and 42 percent for teachers). In the standardization study, it

TABLE 4.8. *The High-Functioning Autism Spectrum Screening Questionnaire* (Ehlers & Gillberg, 1999, pp. 139–138).

This child stands out as different from other children of his/her age in the following ways:	No	Somewhat	Yes
1. is old-fashioned or precocious	[ ]	[ ]	[ ]
2. is regarded as an "eccentric professor" by the other children	[ ]	[ ]	[ ]
3. lives somewhat in a world of his/her own with restricted idiosyncratic intellectual interests	[ ]	[ ]	[ ]
4. accumulates facts on certain subjects (good rote memory), but does not really understand the meaning	[ ]	[ ]	[ ]
5. has a literal understanding of ambiguous and metaphorical language	[ ]	[ ]	[ ]
6. has a deviant style of communication with a formal, fussy, old-fashioned or "robot like" language	[ ]	[ ]	[ ]
7. invents idiosyncratic words and expressions	[ ]	[ ]	[ ]
8. has a different voice or speech	[ ]	[ ]	[ ]
9. expresses sounds involuntarily; clears throat, grunts, smacks, cries or screams	[ ]	[ ]	[ ]
10. is surprisingly good at some things and surprisingly poor at others	[ ]	[ ]	[ ]
11. uses language freely but fails to make adjustment to fit social contexts or the needs of different listeners	[ ]	[ ]	[ ]
12. lacks empathy	[ ]	[ ]	[ ]
13. makes naïve and embarrassing remarks	[ ]	[ ]	[ ]
14. has a deviant style of gaze	[ ]	[ ]	[ ]
15. wishes to be sociable but fails to make relationships with peers	[ ]	[ ]	[ ]
16. can be with other children but only on his/her terms	[ ]	[ ]	[ ]
17. lacks best friend	[ ]	[ ]	[ ]
18. lacks commons sense	[ ]	[ ]	[ ]
19. is poor at games: no idea of cooperating in a team, scores "own goals"	[ ]	[ ]	[ ]
20. has clumsy, ill coordinated, ungainly, awkward movements or gestures	[ ]	[ ]	[ ]
21. has involuntary face or body movements	[ ]	[ ]	[ ]
22. has difficulties in completing simple daily activities because of compulsory repetition of certain actions or thoughts	[ ]	[ ]	[ ]
23. has special routines: insists on no change	[ ]	[ ]	[ ]
24. shows idiosyncratic attachment to objects	[ ]	[ ]	[ ]
25. is bullied by other children	[ ]	[ ]	[ ]
26. has markedly unusual facial expression	[ ]	[ ]	[ ]
27. has markedly unusual posture	[ ]	[ ]	[ ]

Note: Reprinted with kind permission of Springer Science and Business Media. Copyright © 1999 Plenum Publishing Corporation.

was not unusual for children with other disorders (e.g., ADHD and other disruptive behavior disorders) to obtain *ASSQ* scores at this level. This first set of cutoff scores might be used to suggest that a referral for an autism diagnostic assessment, though not immediately indicated, should not be ruled out. In other words, a school psychologist could proceed with a traditional psycho-education evaluation and make referral for a diagnostic assessment for autism only if additional data suggests it to be necessary.

The second set of cutoff scores (parents 19 and teachers 22) were suggested to be the level required to determine the need for an immediate autism diagnostic evaluation among school-aged children in a clinical setting. This set of scores was associated with a false positive rate for parents and teachers of 10 and 9 percent, respectively. In other words, the chances are low that the student who attains this level of ASSQ cutoff scores will not have autism. Of course, on the other hand, this higher cutoff level will increase the risk of false negatives.

The *Childhood Asperger Syndrome Test* (CAST; Scott, Baron-Cohen, Bolton, & Brayne, 2002) is currently being developed as a screening tool for use with mainstream primary grade children (ages 4 through 11 years). A sample of this questionnaire is provided in Table 4.9. This screening has 39 items, with 31 key items contributing to the total score. The eight control items, which assess general development, are numbers 3, 4, 12, 22, 26, 33, 38, and 39. A cutoff score of 15 (out of 31) positive responses to the key items correctly identified 87.5 percent (7 out of 8) of the cases of autistic spectrum disorders. However, the rate of false positives is rather high (36.4 percent). This finding emphasizes the fact that screening tools should not be used diagnostically. Rather they should be considered as tools to assess the need for additional diagnostic assessment. The true false negative rate for this tool has not yet been identified, and a more refined scoring system "with an algorithm for different key difficulties and presentations" is currently being worked on (F.J. Scott, personal communication, February 9, 2004).

The *Australian Scale for Asperger's Syndrome* (A.S.A.S.) is a parent and teacher rating scale found in the book *Asperger's Syndrome: A Guide for Parents and Professionals* by Tony Attwood (1998). A copy of this questionnaire is provided in Table 4.10. It includes 24 items that are rated on a scale of 0 to 5. In addition, it includes 10 behavioral characteristics to be identified as present with a checkmark. According to Attwood (1998): "If the answer is yes to the majority of the questions in the scale, and the rating was between two and six (i.e., conspicuously above the normal range), it does not automatically imply the child has Asperger's Syndrome. However, it is a possibility and a referral for a diagnostic assessment is warranted" (p. 20).

A final screening tool with some promise for use within clinical populations of children age 4 years and older (with mental ages above 2 years of age) is the *Social Communication Questionnaire* (SCQ; Rutter, Bailey, & Lord, 2003; formally known as the *Autism Screening Questionnaire*; Berument, Rutter, Lord, Pickles, & Bailey, 1999). Published by Western Psychological Services, there are two forms of the *SCQ*: a *Lifetime* and a *Current* form. The latter asks questions about the child's behavior in the past 3 months and is suggested to provide data helpful in understanding a child's "everyday living experiences and evaluating treatment and educational plans" (p. 1). The former (*Lifetime*) asks questions about the child's entire developmental history and provides the screening data to be used when determining if a diagnostic assessment is needed.

TABLE 4.9. *Childhood Asperger Syndrome Test* (CAST; Scott et al., 2002, pp. 27–28).

1. Does s/he join in playing games with other children easily?	YES	**NO**
2. Does s/he come up to you spontaneously for a chat?	YES	**NO**
3. Was s/he speaking by 2 years old?	YES	NO
4. Does s/he enjoy sports?	YES	NO
5. Is it important to him/her to fit in with the peer group?	YES	NO
6. Does s/he appear to notice unusual details that others miss?	**YES**	NO
7. Does s/he tend to take things literally?	**YES**	NO
8. When s/he was 3 years old, did s/he spend a lot of time pretending (e.g., play-acting begin a superhero, or holding a teddy's tea parties)?	YES	**NO**
9. Does s/he like to do things over and over again, in the same way all the time?	**YES**	NO
10. Does s/he find it easy to interact with other children?	YES	**NO**
11. Can s/he keep a two-way conversation going?	YES	**NO**
12. Can s/he read appropriately for his/her age?	YES	NO
13. Does s/he mostly have the same interest as his/her peers?	YES	NO
14. Does s/he have an interest, which takes up so much time that s/he does little else?	YES	NO
15. Does s/he have friends, rather than just acquaintances?	YES	NO
16. Does s/he often bring you things s/he is interested in to show you?	YES	NO
17. Does s/he enjoy joking around?	YES	NO
18. Does s/he have difficulty understanding the rules for polite behavior?	YES	NO
19. Does s/he appear to have an unusual memory for details?	YES	NO
20. Is his/her voice unusual (e.g., overly adult, flat, or very monotonous)?	YES	NO
21. Are people important to him/her?	YES	NO
22. Can s/he dress him/herself?	YES	NO
23. Is s/he good at turn taking in conversation?	YES	NO
24. Does s/he play imaginatively with other children, and engage in role-play?	YES	NO
25. Does s/he often do or say things that are tactless or socially inappropriate?	YES	NO
26. Can s/he count to 50 without leaving out any numbers?	YES	NO
27. Does s/he make normal eye-contact?	YES	NO
28. Does s/he have any unusual and repetitive movements?	YES	NO
29. Is his/her social behavior very one-sided and always on his/her own terms?	YES	NO
30. Does s/he sometimes say 'you' or 's/he' when s/he means 'I'?	YES	NO
31. Does s/he prefer imaginative activities such as play-acting or story-telling, rather than numbers or lists of facts?	YES	NO
32. Does s/he sometimes lose the listener because of not explaining what s/he is talking about?	YES	NO
33. Can s/he ride a bicycle (even if with stabilizers)?	YES	NO
34. Does s/he try to impose routines on him/herself, or on others, in such a way that it causes problems?	YES	NO
35. Does s/he care how s/he is perceived by the rest of the group?	YES	NO
36. Does s/he often turn the conversations to his/her favorite subject rather than following what the other person wants to talk about?	YES	NO
37. Does s/he have odd or unusual phrases?	YES	NO

SPECIAL NEEDS SECTION

38. Have teachers/health visitors ever expressed any concerns about his/her development	YES	NO
If Yes, please specify		
39. Has s/he ever been diagnosed with any of the following?		
Language delay	YES	NO
Hyperactivity/Attention Deficit Disorder (ADD)	YES	NO
Hearing or Vision Difficulties	YES	NO

(Cont.)

TABLE 4.9. *Continued*

Autism Spectrum Conditions, incl. Asperger's Syndrome	YES	NO
A physical disability	YES	NO
Other (please specify)	YES	NO

Any other comments

Note: Reprinted with permission from *Autism*. Copyright (©NAS: The National Autistic Society and SAGE Publications Ltd, 2002), by permission of SAGE Publications Ltd.

CAST Scoring Instructions:
University of Cambridge, Social & Communication Development Questionnaire—Key: Autism spectrum disorder relevant responses are indicated in this key and score '1.' Maximum score possible is 31, cutoff currently is 15 for possible autism spectrum disorder or related social-communication difficulties. Questions that are not indicated as having a YES or NO response (3, 4, 12, 22, 26, 33, 38, and 39) are controls.

1. No	6. Yes	11. No	16. No	21. No	26.	31. No	36. Yes
2. No	7. Yes	12.	17. No	22.	27. No	32. Yes	37. Yes
3.	8. No	13. No	18. Yes	23. No	28. Yes	33.	38.
4.	9. Yes	14. Yes	19. Yes	24. No	29. Yes	34. Yes	39.
5. No	10. No	15. No	20. Yes	25. Yes	30. Yes	35. No	

Note: Scoring Key adapted with permission from the Autism Research Centre, University of Cambridge. Copyright © Autism Research Centre.

The *SCQ* consists of 40 Yes/No questions asked of the parent. The first item of this questionnaire documents the child's ability to speak and is used to determine which items will be used in calculating the total score (i.e., if the child has speech *SCQ* items 2 through 40 are used, and if the child does not items 8 through 40 are used). An "AutoScore" protocol converts the parents' Yes/No responses to scores of 1 or 0. The manual reports that in the standardization sample the mean *SCQ* score of children with autism was 24.2, whereas the general population mean was 5.2. To minimize the rate of false negatives, the authors selected a score of 15 or higher as the threshold reflecting the need for diagnostic assessment. However, they caution that a slightly lower threshold might be appropriate if other risk factors (e.g., the child being screened is the sibling of a person with autism) are present. In addition, it is important to note that the authors of this measure acknowledge that more data is needed to determine the frequency of false negatives (Rutter et al., 2003).

Although it is not particularly effective at distinguishing among various autism spectrum disorders, the *SCQ* has been found to have good discriminative validity between autism and other disorders including non-autistic mild or moderate mental retardation. Thus, this tool would appear useful for the school psychologist working with primary grade special needs students (i.e., young school-aged clinical populations; Rutter et al., 2003).

TABLE 4.10. *Australian Scale for Asperger's Syndrome* (A.S.A.S.; Attwood, 1998, pp. 17–19).

A. Social and Emotional Abilities

1. Does the child lack an understanding of how to play with other children? For example, unaware of the unwritten rules of social play.

0	1	2	3	4	5	6

Rarely   Frequently

2. When free to play with other children, such as school lunchtime, does the child avoid social contact with them? For example, finds a secluded place or goes to the library.

0	1	2	3	4	5	6

Rarely   Frequently

3. Does the child appear unaware of social conventions or codes of conduct and make inappropriate actions and comments? For example, making a personal comment to someone but the child seems unaware how the comment could offend.

0	1	2	3	4	5	6

Rarely   Frequently

4. Does the child lack empathy, i.e., The intuitive understanding of another person's feelings? For example, not realizing an apology would help the other person feel better.

0	1	2	3	4	5	6

Rarely   Frequently

5. Does the child seem to expect other people to know their thoughts, experiences and opinions? For example, not realizing you could not know about something because you were not with the child at the time.

0	1	2	3	4	5	6

Rarely   Frequently

6. Does the child need an excessive amount of reassurance, especially if things are changed or go wrong?

0	1	2	3	4	5	6

Rarely   Frequently

7. Does the child lack subtlety in their expression of emotion? For example, the child shows distress of affection out of proportion to the situation.

0	1	2	3	4	5	6

Rarely   Frequently

8. Does the child lack precision in their expression of emotion? For example, not understanding the levels of emotional expression appropriate for different people.

0	1	2	3	4	5	6

Rarely   Frequently

9. Is the child not interested in participating in competitive sports, games and activities?

0	1	2	3	4	5	6

Rarely   Frequently

10. Is the child *indifferent* to peer pressure? For example, does *not* follow the latest craze in toys or clothes.

0	1	2	3	4	5	6

B. Communication Abilities

Rarely   Frequently

11. Does the child take a literal interpretation of comments? For example, is confused by phrases such as 'pull your socks up', 'looks can kill', or 'hop on the scales'.

0	1	2	3	4	5	6

Rarely   Frequently

12. Does the child have an unusual tone of voice? For example, the child seems to have a 'foreign' accent or monotone that lacks emphasis on key words.

0	1	2	3	4	5	6

(Cont.)

TABLE 4.10. *Continued*

13.	When talking to the child does he or she appear uninterested in your side of the conversation? For example, not asking about or commenting on your thoughts or opinions on the topic.	Rarely 0 1 2 3 4 5 6 Frequently

14.	When in a conversation, does the child tend to use less eye contact than you would expect?	Rarely 0 1 2 3 4 5 6 Frequently

15.	Is the child's speech over-precise or pedantic? For example, talks in a formal way or like a walking dictionary.	Rarely 0 1 2 3 4 5 6 Frequently

16.	Does the child have problems repairing a conversation? For example, when the child is confused, he or she does not ask for clarification but simply switches to a familiar topic, or takes ages to think of a reply.	Rarely 0 1 2 3 4 5 6 Frequently

C. Cognitive Skills

17.	Does the child read books primarily for information, not seeming to be interested in fictional works? For example, being an avid reader of encyclopedias and science books but not keen on adventure stories.	Rarely 0 1 2 3 4 5 6 Frequently

18.	Does the child have an exceptional long-term memory for events and facts? For example, remembering the neighbour's car registration of several years ago, or clearly recalling scenes that happened many years ago.	Rarely 0 1 2 3 4 5 6 Frequently

19.	Does the child lack social imaginative play? For example, other children are not included in the child's imaginary games or the child is confused by pretend games of other children.	Rarely 0 1 2 3 4 5 6 Frequently

D. Specific Interests

20.	Is the child fascinated by a particular topic and avidly collects information or statistics on that interest? For example, the child becomes a walking encyclopedia of knowledge on vehicles, maps or league tables.	Rarely 0 1 2 3 4 5 6 Frequently

21.	Does the child become unduly upset by changes in routine or expectation? For example, is distressed by going to school by a different route.	Rarely 0 1 2 3 4 5 6 Frequently

22.	Does the child develop elaborate routines or rituals that must be completed? For example, lining up toys before going to bed.	Rarely 0 1 2 3 4 5 6 Frequently

E. Movement Skills

23.	Does the child have poor motor coordination? For example, is not skilled at catching a ball.	Rarely 0 1 2 3 4 5 6 Frequently

24.	Does the child have an odd gait when running?	Rarely 0 1 2 3 4 5 6 Frequently

TABLE 4.10. *Continued*

F. Other Characteristics

For this section, tick whether the child has shown any of the following characteristics.

(a) Unusual fear or distress due to ☐
   ○ ordinary sounds, e.g. electrical appliances ☐
   ○ light touch on skin or scalp ☐
   ○ wearing particular items of clothing ☐
   ○ unexpected noises ☐
   ○ seeing certain objects ☐
   ○ noisy, crowded places, e.g. supermarkets ☐
(b) A tendency to flap or rock when excited or distressed ☐
(c) A lack of sensitivity to low levels of pain ☐
(d) Late in acquiring speech ☐
(e) Unusual facial grimaces or tics ☐

Note: Reprinted with permission from Tony Attwood. Co-authored by Michelle Garnett. Copyright ©
1998 Tony Attwood.

Concluding Comments

The increasing incidence of autism, combined with the importance of early identification creates the need for all school professionals to become better prepared
to identify these disorders. With appropriate intervention, there is hope that the
student with autism will be able to achieve a significant degree of independent
functioning. These interventions, however, can only be provided if the student
with autism is identified and case finding and screening are the first steps in the
identification process.

Although much progress has been made in the early identification of autism, it
needs to be recognized that the currently available screening tools are not perfect,
and that some children who are suggested to not have autism by the available case
finding and screening techniques will go on to eventually be diagnosed with one of
these disorders. Thus, as illustrated in Figure 4.1, when a screening is not indicated
it will be important to continue to monitor development. Further, in some cases,
even when screening tests are negative for autism, there may be a need to refer for
assessments and to continue to monitor development.

5
Diagnostic Assessment

As illustrated in Chapter 4, Figure 4.1, screening test results should be used to determine if an autism diagnostic assessment is required. When such diagnostic assessments are indicated, it is important to keep in mind that no single test will reliably identify these disorders (Neuwirth & Segal, 1997). Thus, diagnostic assessments require multiple methods employed across multiple settings by a multidisciplinary team of specialists (Tidmarsh & Volkmar, 2003).

Although the diagnostic process should include a variety of specialists from a variety of disciplines [e.g., psychiatry, neurology, pediatrics, occupational therapy, speech pathology, and special education (Filipek et al., 1999)], one treatment provider (often a psychologist) should be designated to coordinate the assessment (Deisinger, 2001). When a specific *Diagnostic and Statistical Manual of Mental Disorders* [Fourth Edition, Text Revision (DSM IV-TR); American Psychiatric Association (APA), 2000] diagnosis is being sought, whether or not a school psychologist takes on this coordination role should be determined by the individual's prior training and supervised practice.

Making a *DSM IV-TR* diagnosis requires special clinical training and supervised practice, and *only those school professionals with appropriate training and supervision should diagnose autism.* In fact, according to the National Research Council (2001): "The level of expertise required for effective diagnosis and assessment may require the services of individuals, or a team of individuals, other than those usually available in a school setting" (p. 26). The minimal professional requirements needed to diagnosis an autism spectrum disorder, as defined by the California Department of Developmental Services, are provided in Table 5.1.

Regardless of whether a school psychologist meets these standards, it will be important for him or her to know the elements of an autism diagnosis so as to be better able to support this process. In addition, while it is the *Individuals with Disabilities Education Act* (IDEA), and not *DSM IV-TR,* that drive, special education eligibility determinations, published case law does reveal hearing officers and judges to consider *DSM IV-TR* diagnostic criteria in just over half of their rulings addressing special education eligibility decisions (Fogt, Miller, & Zirkel, 2003). Thus, knowledge of how to make a *DSM IV-TR* autism diagnosis is important.

TABLE 5.1. California Department of Developmental Services (2002, pp. 6–7) guidelines for the minimal professional development required to diagnose autism.

1. Qualification to render a diagnosis of autistic spectrum disorder (ASD) under the provision of California state licensure.
2. Documented appropriate and specific supervision and training in ASD as well as experience in the diagnosis of ASD. This would include the following:
   a. Graduate and/or postgraduate studies in a psychology, education and/or child development program with particular emphasis in developmental disabilities, including autism and related neurodevelopmental disorders

AND

   b. Supervised experience in a graduate training program (e. g. predoctoral, postdoctoral) in a clinic and/or treatment setting serving children with ASD. Specific residency or fellowship training should have specific didactic training and clinical experience in the diagnosis and treatment of ASD. This would necessarily include training in the diagnosis of ASD as well as the administration of measurement tools specific to ASD.

OR

   c. Documented fellowship in a credentialed medical training program in pediatrics, child neurology or child psychiatry. This would extend beyond the typical four week rotation through developmental/pediatrics in general pediatric training, which encompasses a broad range of developmental difficulties in addition to autism. Specific residency or fellowship training should have specific didactic training and clinical experience in the diagnosis and treatment of ASD.
3. Clinical experience with the variability within the ASD population as well as extensive knowledge of typical child development.

Providing such information is the goal of this chapter. To obtain this goal, discussion will first provide a review of diagnostic criteria. Then, the developmental, health, and family history elements of diagnosis are reviewed. Next indirect assessment methods (i.e., rating scales and interview) are examined; and finally, direct behavioral observation assessment strategies are discussed.

Diagnostic Criteria

As was mentioned in Chapter 1, autism includes several diagnostic categories found in the *DSM IV-TR* (APA, 2000). The diagnostic criteria for Autistic Disorder are provided in Table 5.2. For a more detailed discussion refer to Filipek and colleagues (1999), who provide an excellent description of these criteria. As was illustrated in Chapter 1, Figure 1.2, when considering these symptoms it is important to acknowledge that they exist on a continuum. As movement occurs along this continuum from most to least severe, the degree of mental retardation typically associated with autism lessens, and the prognosis of a positive adult outcome increases.

The criteria for Asperger's Disorder (Table 5.3) are essentially the same as Autistic Disorder with the exception that there are no criteria for a qualitative impairment in communication. In fact, Asperger's criteria require "...no clinically significant general delay in language (e.g., single words used by 2 years,

TABLE 5.2. *DSM IV-TR* diagnostic criteria for autistic disorder (APA, 2000, p. 75).

A. A total of six (or more) items for (1), (2), and (3), with at least two from (1), and one each for (2) and (3):

   (1) qualitative impairment in social interaction, as manifested by at least two of the following:

      (a) marked impairment in the use of multiple nonverb..' behaviors such as eye-to-eye gaze, facial expression, body postures, and gestures to regulate social interaction

      (b) failure to develop peer relationships appropriate to developmental level

      (c) a lack of spontaneous seeking to share enjoyment, interests, or achievements with other people (e.g., by lack of showing, bringing, or pointing out objects of interest)

      (d) lack of social or emotional reciprocity

   (2) qualitative impairments in communication as manifested by at least one of the following:

      (a) delay in, or total lack of, the development of spoken language (not accompanied by an attempt to compensate through alternative modes of communication such as gesture or mime)

      (b) in individuals with adequate speech, marked impairment in the ability to initiate or sustain a conversation with others

      (c) stereotyped and repetitive use of language or idiosyncratic language

      (d) lack of varied, spontaneous make-believe play or social imitative play appropriate to developmental level

   (3) restricted repetitive and stereotyped patterns of behavior, interests, and activities, as manifested by at least one of the following:

      (a) encompassing preoccupation with one or more stereotyped and restricted patterns of interest that is abnormal either in intensity or focus

      (b) apparently inflexible adherence to specific, nonfunctional routines or rituals

      (c) stereotyped and repetitive motor mannerisms (e.g., hand or finger flapping or twisting, or complex whole-body movements)

      (d) persistent preoccupation with parts of objects

B. Delays or abnormal functioning in at least one of the following areas, with onset prior to age 3 years: (1) social interaction, (2) language as used in social communication, or (3) symbolic or imaginative play.

C. The disturbance is not better accounted for by Rett's Disorder or Childhood Disintegrative Disorder.

Note: Reprinted with permission from the Diagnostic and Statistical Manual of Mental Disorders, Fourth Edition, Text Revision (Copyright © 2000), American Psychiatric Association.

communicative phrases used by 3 years;" APA, 2000, p. 84). The criteria for Childhood Disintegrative Disorder (Table 5.4) are also essentially the same as Autistic Disorder. Differences between criteria include that in the former there has been (a) "Apparently normal development for at least the first 2 years after birth as manifested by the presence of age-appropriate verbal and nonverbal communication, social relationships, play, and adaptive behavior" (p. 79); and that there is (b) "Clinically significant loss of previously acquired skills (before age 10 years) in at least two of the following areas: (1) expressive or receptive language; (2) social skills or adaptive behavior; (3) bowel or bladder control; (4) play; (5) motor-skills" (p. 79).

As was mention earlier, the diagnostic criteria for Rett's Disorder, which occurs primarily among females, are relatively distinct. These criteria are provided in

TABLE 5.3. *DSM IV-TR* diagnostic criteria for Asperger's Disorder (APA, 2000, p. 84).

A. Qualitative impairment in social interaction, as manifested by at least two of the following
  (1) marked impairment in the use of multiple nonverbal behaviors such as eye-to-eye gaze, facial expression, body postures, and gestures to regulate social interaction
  (2) failure to develop peer relationships appropriate to developmental level
  (3) a lack of spontaneous seeking to share enjoyment, interests, or achievements with other people (e.g., by lack of showing, bringing, or pointing out objects of interest)
  (4) lack of social or emotional reciprocity
B. Restricted repetitive and stereotyped patterns of behavior, interests, and activities, as manifested by at least one of the following:
  (1) encompassing preoccupation with one or more stereotyped and restricted patterns of interest that is abnormal either in intensity or focus
  (2) apparently inflexible adherence to specific, nonfunctional routines or rituals
  (3) stereotyped and repetitive motor mannerisms (e.g., hand or finger flapping or twisting, or complex whole-body movements)
  (4) persistent preoccupation with parts of objects
C. The disturbance causes clinically significant impairment in social, occupational, or other important areas of functioning.
D. There is no clinically significant delay in cognitive development or in the development of age-appropriate self-help skills, adaptive behavior (other than in social interaction), and curiosity about the environment in childhood.
E. Criteria are not met for another Pervasive Developmental Disorder or Schizophrenia.

Note: Reprinted with permission from the Diagnostic and Statistical Manual of Mental Disorders, Fourth Edition, Text Revision (Copyright © 2000), American Psychiatric Association.

TABLE 5.4. *DSM IV-TR* diagnostic criteria for Childhood Disintegrative Disorder (APA, 2000, p. 79).

A. Apparently normal development for at least the first 2 years after birth as manifested by the presence of age-appropriate verbal and nonverbal communication, social relationships, play, and adaptive behavior.
B. Clinically significant loss of previously acquired skills (before 10 years) in at least two of the following areas:
  (1) expressive or receptive language
  (2) social skills or adaptive behavior
  (3) bowel or bladder control
  (4) play
  (5) motor skills
C. Abnormalities of functions in at least two of the following areas:
  (1) qualitative impairment in social interaction (e.g., impairment in nonverbal behaviors, failure to develop peer relationships, lack of social or emotional reciprocity)
  (2) qualitative impairments in communication (e.g., delay or lack of spoken language, inability to initiate or sustain a conversation, stereotyped and repetitive use of language, lack of varied make-believe play)
  (3) restricted, repetitive, and stereotyped patterns of behavior, interests, and activities, including motor stereotypes and movements
D. The disturbance is not better accounted for by another specific Pervasive Developmental Disorder or by Schizophrenia.

Note: Reprinted with permission from the Diagnostic and Statistical Manual of Mental Disorders, Fourth Edition, Text Revision (Copyright © 2000), American Psychiatric Association.

TABLE 5.5. *DSM IV-TR* diagnostic criteria for Rett's Disorder (APA, 2000, p. 77).

A. All of the following:
    (1) apparently normal prenatal and perinatal development
    (2) apparently normal psychomotor development
    (3) normal head circumference at birth
B. Onset of all of the following after the period or normal development:
    (1) deceleration of head growth between ages 5 and 48 months
    (2) loss of previously acquired purposeful hand skills between ages 5 and 30 months
    (3) loss of social engagement early in the course (although often social interaction develops later)
    (4) appearance of poorly coordinated gait or trunk movements
    (5) severely impaired expressive and receptive language development with severe psychomotor retardation

Note: Reprinted with permission from the Diagnostic and Statistical Manual of Mental Disorders, Fourth Edition, Text Revision (Copyright © 2000). American Psychiatric Association.

Table 5.5. Comparison of Autistic Disorder and Rett's Disorder criteria (Tables 5.2 and 5.5) reveals that both include delays in expressive and receptive language development and social engagement (although as was mentioned earlier, the social difficulties may not be as pervasive). However, unlike Autistic Disorder, Rett's also includes (a) head growth deceleration between the ages of five months and four years, (b) loss of fine motor skill, (c) poorly coordinated gross motor skill, and (d) severe psychomotor retardation (APA, 2000; Deisinger, 2001).

Symptom onset. Autistic Disorder diagnostic criteria require symptom onset before the age of three years. Onset may be somewhat later for Asperger's Disorder, with no specific age specified. In fact, *DSM IV-TR* (APA, 2000) reports that parents of children with Asperger's Disorder may not have been concerned about their child's early development. Autistic Disorder criteria specify that before age three years, their must be "delays or abnormal functioning" in at least one of the following areas: (a) social interaction, (b) social communicative language, and/or (c) symbolic or imaginative play (APA, 2000, p. 75). Early social interaction difficulties may include:

- acting as if unaware of the coming and going of others (vs. crying when the mother leaves the room or becoming anxious with strangers);
- appearing inaccessible, as if in a shell (vs. recognizing and smiling at familiar faces);
- begin indifferent or finding aversive physical contact (vs. enjoying being held and cuddled; APA, 2000; Neuwirth & Segal, 1997).

Early social communicative language difficulties may include:

- avoiding eye contact (vs. studying the mother's face);
- not responding to parents voice and appearing to be deaf (vs. being easily stimulated by and appearing to recognize sounds);

- lack of facial responsivity and socially directed smiling (vs. responding with a range of affect to pleasant social stimuli);
- starting to develop language and then abruptly stopping (vs. continuous growth in vocabulary and grammar); and
- not being able to ask for something or indicate an interest (vs. being able to point to and ask for a desired object or to indicate an interest (APA, 2000; Baron-Cohen et al., 2000; Neuwirth & Segal, 1997).

Finally, early symbolic or imaginative play difficulties may include the failure to engage in pretend games (versus, for example, being able to pretend to make a cup of tea with a toy cup and teapot; Baron-Cohen et al., 2000).

Onset criteria for Childhood Disintegrative Disorder requires symptom onset before the age of 10 years (preceded by at least two years of normal development), while Rett's Disorder requires symptom onset before the age of 4 years (although symptoms are usually seen by the second year of life).

Developmental course. DSM IV-TR (APA, 2000) criteria for Autistic Disorder states: "In some instances, parents will report that they have been worried about the child since birth or shortly afterward because of the child's lack of interest in social interaction" (p. 73). However, this manual also indicates that while there is typically no period of "normal development," in a few cases it is reported that the child initially developed normally before Autistic Disorder symptom onset. However, for this diagnosis to be made, such periods of normal development must not extend past age three. This requirement does not mean that the diagnosis must be made before the age of three. It can even be made in much later in life if the diagnostician is able to verify that symptoms were present before the cutoff age. The duration of Autistic Disorder is typically lifelong, with only a small percentage being able to live and work independently. Adult outcome is especially poor for those individuals with IQs *below* 50. In a study of individuals with IQs *above* 50, it was found that a majority of adults achieved some degree of independent functioning. Although having a performance IQ above 70 was associated with a significantly better adult outcome, even this group included individuals whose symptoms continue to cause significant challenges (Howlin, Goode, Hutton, & Rutter, 2004).

Criteria for Asperger's Disorder suggest that motor delays or clumsiness may be some of the first symptoms noted during the preschool years, with difficulties in social interactions becoming apparent as the child enters the school setting. Also noted at about the time of school entry are symptoms associated with unique and unusually circumscribed interests (Baird, Cass, & Slonims, 2003). As is the case for Autistic Disorder, the duration of Asperger's Disorder is typically lifelong with difficulties empathizing and modulating social interactions being characteristic of this disorder in adulthood (APA, 2000). However, the degree of independent functioning in adulthood is typically greater than that seen among individuals with Autistic Disorder.

Both Rett's and Childhood Disintegrative Disorders are lifelong conditions. Rett's distinctive pattern of developmental regression is generally persistent and progressive. However, some interest in social interaction may be noted during later childhood and adolescence. The "insidious or abrupt" (APA, 2000, p. 78) loss of skills associated with Childhood Disintegrative Disorder usually reaches a plateau after which some limited improvement may occur. Warning signs of symptom onset may include "increased activity levels, irritability, and anxiety followed by a loss of speech and other skills" (APA, 2000, p. 78). Due to their association with severe to profound mental retardation the adult outcome for these disorders is worse that that associated with Autistic Disorder (Edelson, 1995; Yale Child Study Center, n.d.).

Associated features. Asperger's Disorder is the only autism spectrum disorder that is not typically associated with some degree of mental retardation. Autistic Disorder is commonly associated with moderate mental retardation, and Child-hood Disintegrative Disorder is usually associated with severe mental retardation. Children with Rett's Disorder are as a rule the most cognitively impaired with se-vere to profound mental retardation being typical. Other features associated with Autistic Disorder include a range of ADHD-like behavioral symptoms, unusual sensory sensitivities (e.g., being oversensitive to some stimuli and being unusu-ally interested in others), abnormal eating or sleeping habits, unusual fearfulness of harmless objects or lack of fear of real dangers, and self-injurious behaviors (APA, 2000).

Age-specific features. As discussed in Chapter 4, the chronological age and de-velopmental level of the child will influence the expression of Autistic Disorder. Thus, assessment must be developmentally sensitive. For example, the *DSM IV-TR* specifies that among infants "there may be a failure to cuddle; an indifference or aversion to affection or physical contact; a lack of eye contact, facial responsive-ness, or socially directed smiles; and a failure to respond to their parents' voices" (APA, 2000, p. 72). In contrast, among young children, adults may be treated as interchangeable or alternatively the young child may "cling mechanically to a spe-cific person" (APA, 2000, p. 73). They may prefer to be alone, not show emotion upon separation from or reunification with parents, become upset with changes in routine or environment, and demonstrate echolalic speech, odd repetitive motor behavior, and unusual attachments to objects. As a child progresses through child-hood, failure to make friends or display social/emotional reciprocity is observed. By middle childhood, the person with autism will rarely share interests with others and will demonstrate limited social and verbal expression and social interactions. Finally, in adolescence the individual may have few if any friends and often fail to understand social rules and conventions. Unusual affect, persistent and repetitive speech and/or behaviors are also observed (Jelline, Patel, & Froehle, 2002).

Gender-related features. With the exception of Rett's Disorder, which occurs pri-marily among females, all other autism spectrum disorders appear to be more com-mon among males than females. The rate of Autistic Disorder is four to five times higher in males than in females. However, it is noted that females with Autistic Disorder are more likely to exhibit more severe mental retardation (APA, 2000).

TABLE 5.6. Differential diagnosis of Autistic Disorder.

Disorder	Differentiating features from Autistic Disorder
Rett's Disorder	• Typically affects only girls • Head growth deceleration • Loss of fine motor (hand) skill • Hand wringing • Awkward gait and trunk movement • Mutations in the MECP2 gene (on the X chromosome)
Childhood Disintegrative Disorder	• Regression following at least two years of normal development
Asperger's Disorder	• Language development is not delayed • Normal intelligence, more abstract thinking • Later symptom onset • Gross and fine motor problems
Schizophrenia	• Years of normal or near normal development • Symptoms of hallucinations and delusions
Selective mutism	• Normal language in certain situations/settings • No restricted patterns of behavior
Language disorders	• No severe impairment of social interactions • No restricted patterns of behavior
Attention-deficit/Hyperactivity Disorder	• Distractible inattention related to external (not internal) stimuli • Deterioration in attention and vigilance over time
Mental retardation	• Relative to developmental level, social interactions are not severely impaired • No restricted patterns of behavior
Obsessive Compulsive Disorder	• Normal language and communication skills • Normal social skills
Reactive Attachment Disorder	• History of severe neglect and/or abuse • Social deficits dramatically remit in response to environmental change

Note: Sources APA (2000), Filipek et al. (1999), Hendren (2003), National Research Council (2001), Rau (2003).

According to Attwood (1998), the male to female ratio for Asperger's Disorder is the same as that for Autistic disorder.

Differential diagnosis. Finally, the autism diagnostic requirements require that other conditions with similar symptoms be ruled out before an autism diagnosis is made (Neuwirth & Segal, 1997). The diagnostic differences between other disorders (including the other autism spectrum disorders) and Autistic Disorder, which need to be considered and ruled out when making the diagnosis of Autistic Disorder, are summarized in Table 5.6. Recent research has also identified negative symptoms or deficits that differentiate autism from other developmental disorders. The symptoms which are apparent in the 20- to 36-month age range include deficits in (a) eye contact, (b) orienting to name, (c) joint attention (e.g., sharing or bringing something to someone else attention), (d) pretend play, (e) imitation, and (f) verbal and nonverbal language development (Filipek et al., 1999).

Developmental, Health, and Family History

The first step of the diagnostic assessment process is to review with parents their child's developmental and health history (Deisinger, 2001; Goodwin-Jones & Solomon, 2003; Shriver, Allen, & Mathews, 1999). The following discussion highlights factors that would support an autism diagnosis. Given that a developmental and health history is typically a part of any psychoeducational evaluation, it is important for all school psychologists to be aware of these factors, and such data collection may be a part of the psychoeducational evaluation. Figure 5.1 provides an interview form that could be used when collecting this information.

Pre-, peri-, and postnatal risk factors. Although the available data have not provided conclusive evidence regarding a causal role for these factors in the development of autism, they at the very least represent additive brain trauma to children already vulnerable for autism and as such are important to consider and understand (Hansen & Hagerman, 2003). Pre- and perinatal factors implicated in an increased risk for autism include greater maternal age at the time of pregnancy, maternal infections (such as measles, mumps, rubella, influenza, cytomegalovirus, herpes, syphilis, and HIV), and drug exposure (Newschaffer, Fallin, & Lee, 2002). For example, the drugs thalidomide and valproate (an anticonvulsant and mood-stabilizer) when taken early in pregnancy have been reported to be associated with autism (Hansen & Hagerman, 2003; Newschaffer et al., 2002). In particular, thalidomide when taken at 20 to 24 weeks gestation is positively correlated with autism risk (Newschaffer et al., 2002).

Given the suggestion that there is some prenatal initiation of the changes associated with the development of autism, and that there is not a strong relationship between any specific factor and autism, one approach has been to look at summary measures of "optimality" of the pregnancy and delivery and to consider "suboptimality" as supportive of a possible autism diagnosis (Newschaffer et al., 2002). A recent population-based study in Western Australia generated results consistent with this suggestion. When compared with a population-based random sample of 1,313 controls and to 481 siblings of individuals with autism, the 465 cases of individuals with autism were significantly more likely to have had obstetric difficulties during pregnancy, labor, delivery, and the neonatal period. Threatened miscarriage and increased maternal age were the strongest findings. However, study authors add that it is unlikely that any single factor or event causes autism. Rather they suggest that the increased prevalence of these complications is likely due to underlying genetic factors or an interaction of these factors with the environment (Glasson et al., 2004).

Postnatal risk factors include infections. For example, several case studies have documented sudden onset of autism symptoms in older children after herpes encephalitis. Other infections that can result in secondary hydrocephalus, such as

COLLEGE OF EDUCATION
DEPARTMENT OF SPECIAL EDUCATION, REHABILITATION
AND SCHOOL PSYCHOLOGY

CALIFORNIA STATE UNIVERSITY,
SACRAMENTO

School Psychology Diagnostic Clinic
6000 J Street
Sacramento, California 95819-6079

AUTISM DIAGNOSTIC EVALUATION
HEALTH, FAMILY, DEVELOPMENTAL, & BEHAVIORAL HISTORY INTERVIEW FORM

Child's Name: _____   Birth date: _____

School: _____   Grade: _____

Parent(s): _____   E-mail: _____

Home phone: _____   Alt. Phone: _____

Languages spoken in the home: _____

Siblings and their ages: _____

Other adults living in the home: _____

Referring concern: _____
_____
_____
_____
_____
_____

At what age did the referring concerns first emerge? _____

Health History (Perinatal Factors)

1. General obstetric status (circle one):   Optimal   Adequate   Poor

2. Mothers age time of the pregnancy (list):   _____

3. Length of pregnancy (circle/list):   Full term   Premature @ _____ weeks

4. Was there threatened miscarriage (circle)?   YES   NO   If YES describe below:

_____
_____
_____

5. Maternal illnesses during the pregnancy
    (circle all that apply/list when illness   Measles _____ Mumps _____ Rubella _____
    occurred):   Influenza _____ Syphilis _____ Herpes _____
                                                 HIV _____   Cytomegalovirus _____
                                                 Other (list): _____
                                                 _____
                                                 _____
                                                 _____

6. Alcohol exposure during pregnancy (circle): YES   NO   If YES answer the following:
    a.   How often did mother drink?   Every day   Once a week   Rarely
    b.   How much did mother drink?   Just a little One drink   Several drinks
    c.   When during pregnancy did
         mother drink?   1st trimester 2nd Trimester 3rd trimester

FIGURE 5.1. This form could be used when collecting health, family, developmental, and behavioral history regarding a child suspected to have autism.

7. Drug exposure during pregnancy (circle):   YES   NO   If YES answer the following:
    a.   What drugs were taken?   Thalidomide   Depakene   Depakote   Depacon
                                     Other (list): _____

    b.   When during pregnancy were
                drugs taken?   1st trimester   2nd Trimester 3rd trimester

8. Complications during delivery (circle)?   YES   NO   If YES answer the following:
    a.   What complications?   Respiratory distress
                                       Meconium aspiration
                                       Other (list): _____

    b.   C-section   YES   NO   Planned   Emergency
    c.   1-min. Apgar   (list): _____
    d.   5-min. Apgar   (list): _____
    e.   10-min. Apgar (list): _____

9. Birth weight (list):   _____lbs.   _____oz.

10. Length (list):   _____inches

Health History (Infancy and Childhood)

11. Head circumference (list):   _____inches at birth   _____%ile at birth
                               _____inches at 1 year   _____%ile at 1 year
                               _____inches at 2 years   _____%ile at 2 years
                               _____inches at 3 years   _____%ile at 3 years
                               _____inches at 4 years   _____%ile at 4 years
                               _____inches at 5 years   _____%ile at 5 years

12. Childhood infections (circle all that   Meningitis ____   Encephalitis ____
    (apply/list when illness occurred)?   Other (list): _____

13. Childhood viruses (circle all that   Mumps Chicken pox ____ Ear infections _____
    Apply/list when illness occurred)?   Unexplained fever   Other (list): _____

14. Medical Diagnoses/Issues (circle):   Tuberous sclerosis   Fragile X syndrome
                                      Fetal alcohol syndrome Epilepsy
                                      Lead poisoning   Pica
                                        Chronic ear infections Tube placement
                                      Immune dysfunction   Thyroid problems
                                        Arthritis   Rashes
                                        Allergy history   Gastrointestinal symptoms
                                      Hydrocephalus   Cerebral palsy
                                      Mental retardation   Other (list): _____

15. Vision Screening (list):   Date: _____   Near 20/___   Far 20/___

FIGURE 5.1. *continued*

16. Suspected hearing loss   YES   NO   If YES describe reasons for concern: _____
_____

17. Hearing Screening (list):   Date: _____   Result: _____

Family History

18. Siblings with autism (circle)?   YES   NO   If YES answer the following:
    a.   Is sibling an identical twin?   YES   NO

19. Siblings with autism-like behavior (circle)?   YES   NO   If YES answer the following:
    a.   Is sibling an identical twin?   YES   NO

20. Family members with autism (circle)?   YES   NO   If YES answer the following:
    a.   Relationship to child (list): _____

21. Family members with autism-like behavior (circle)?   YES   NO   If YES answer the following:
    a.   Relationship to child (list): _____

21. Other health/developmental problems among family members (circle)?   Epilepsy   Mental rctardation
     Other (list): _____
_____
_____
_____

22. Family history of genetic disorders   Tuberous sclerosis   Fragile X syndrome
     Schizophrenia   Anxiety
     Bipolar disorder   Depression
     Other (list): _____
_____
_____
_____

Developmental History

23. Age major milestones were obtained (list)?   First word   _____
     Sentences   _____
     Stands alone   _____
     First steps   _____
     Walks alone   _____

24. Developmental regression observed (circle)?   YES   NO   If YES answer the following:
    a.   Age regression observed (list): _____
    b.   Describe the regression (list): _____
_____
_____

Behavioral History

25. Unusual sensory sensitivities (circle)?   YES   NO   If YES answer the following:
    a.   Over sensitive to stimuli (list): _____
_____
    b.   Unusually interested in stimuli: (list): _____
_____

FIGURE 5.1. *continued*

Behavioral History (continued)

26. Abnormal eating or sleeping habits (list): _____
_____
_____
_____

27. Unusual fearfulness of harmless object (list):_____
_____
_____
_____

28. Lack of fear for real dangers (list): _____
_____
_____
_____

29. Self-injurious behaviors (list): _____
_____
_____

30. Socialization questions (adapted from Filipek et al., 1999):
     Does the child…
          a. cuddle like other children? _____
          b. look at you when you are talking or playing? _____
          c. smile in response to a smile from others? _____
          d. engage in reciprocal, back-and-forth play? _____
          e. play simple imitation games, such as pat-a-cake or peek-a-boo? ___
          f. show interest in other children? _____

31. Communication questions (adapted from Filipek et al., 1999):
     Does the child…
          a. point with his or her finger? _____
          b. gesture (e.g., nod yes and no)? _____
          c. direct your attention by holding up objects for you to see? _____
          d. show things to people? _____
          e. give inconsistent response to his or her name (or to commands)? ___
          f. use rote, repetitive, or echolalic speech? _____
          g. memorize strings of words or scripts? _____

32. Stereotyped behavior questions (adapted from Filipek et al., 1999):
     Does the child…
          a. have repetitive, stereotyped, or odd motor behavior? _____
          b. have preoccupations or a narrow range of interests? _____
          c. attend more to parts of an object (e.g., the wheels of a toy car)? ___
          d. have limited or absent pretend play? _____
          e. Imitate other people's actions? _____
          f. play with toys in the same exact way every time? _____
          g. appear strongly attached to a specific unusual object(s)? _____

FIGURE 5.1. *continued*

meningitis, have also been implicated in the etiology of autism. In addition, common viral illnesses in the first 18 months of life (e.g., mumps, chickenpox, fever of unknown origin, and ear infection) have been associated with autism risk (Newschaffer et al., 2002).

Recently, the postnatal risk factors of chemical exposure and MMR vaccination have received some attention. However, in both cases the available data does not support the hypothesis that these factors are associated with autism and thus should not be given great diagnostic significance. In particular, regarding MMR vaccinations, Madsen and colleagues (2002) report the results of an epidemiological study that they suggest "provides strong evidence against the hypothesis that MMR vaccination causes autism" (p. 1477).

Developmental milestones. The diagnostic evaluation should also collect information regarding early development. In particular, questions should be asked regarding attainment of major language and social developmental milestones (Deisinger, 2001). In one study of the psychological data available for 164 3- to 15-year-olds with autism, it was found that 67 percent had normal motor and delayed speech milestones (Mayes & Calhoun, 2003). Given the lack of response to speech, it is not surprising for this history to include initial concerns that the child had a hearing loss.

Any indication of developmental regression would be of particular concern. Approximately 25 to 30 percent of children with autism demonstrate obvious stasis and sometimes clear developmental regression between 15 and 21 months of age (Baird, Cass, & Slonims, 2003). As was mentioned above, other behaviors that are characteristic of autism (e.g., atypical play, lack of social interest, repetitive behaviors) typically emerge as somewhat later concerns (Hansen & Hagerman, 2003).

Medical history. According to Hansen and Hagerman (2003): "A complete medical history and review of systems are important, with an emphasis on symptoms relevant to medical conditions known to be related to autism or to proposed etiologies" (p. 100). This might include questions concerning current vision and hearing status, the occurrence of chronic ear infections (and tube placement), immune dysfunction (e.g., frequent infections), autoimmune disorders (e.g., thyroid problems, arthritis, rashes), allergy history (e.g., to foods or environmental triggers), and gastrointestinal symptoms (e.g., diarrhea, constipation, bloating, abdominal pain).

Diagnostic history. A diagnostic history should be gathered as autism is sometimes observed in association with other neurological or general medical conditions (Deisinger, 2001). According to the APA (2000), these conditions include encephalitis, phenylketonuria, tuberous sclerosis, and fragile X syndrome. Tharp (2003) reports that 10 to 20 percent of children with autism have a neurodevelopmental genetic syndrome. Specifically, mental retardation is found in up to 80 percent, tuberous sclerosis is in 2 to 4 percent, and fragile X syndrome in 2 to 8 percent of children with autism. In particular, epilepsy is found in 3 to 30 percent of children with autism, with EEG abnormalities being common even in the absence of seizure disorders. It is also significant to note that seizures may develop (particularly in adolescence) in as many as 25 percent of children with autism (APA, 2000; Hansen & Hagerman, 2003). If this information is not already available, a medical assessment may be indicated, and Table 5.7 provides a list of medical procedures that might be conducted as part of an autism diagnostic evaluation.

Family history. Finally, a family history of any autism spectrum disorder would support an autism diagnosis. According to Newschaffer and colleagues (2002): "Evidence from twin studies, familial aggregation, and rare chromosomal

TABLE 5.7. Medical assessments that may be part of the autism diagnostic evaluation.

- Audiological examination (especially if there are concerns about language delay)[a]
- Tests for lead poisoning (especially if there is a history of pica)[a]
- Growth measurements (especially head circumference)
- A neurological examination and as indicated EEG and MRI
- Examination of skin using a Wood's light for skin markings consistent with tuberous sclerosis
- Laboratory investigations, which may include tests for:
  - Fragile X
  - Chromosome analysis
  - Rett's gene
  - Thyroid and PKU
  - Blood count or film for iron deficiency (especially when dietary habits are limited)

Source: Adapted from Baird, Cass, & Slonims (2003); Rau (2003); Tidmarsh & Volkmar (2003).
Note: [a]Recommended as part of any autism screening by Filipek et al. (1999).

abnormalities provide a compelling argument for some substantive heritable components in autism's etiology. However, no specific genes have been implicated" (p. 143). A family history of other conditions associated with autism might also provide some support for an autism diagnosis. These conditions include acquired epilepsy, mental retardation, and conditions with a genetic basis (e.g., tuberous sclerosis complex, Fragile X Syndrome, schizophrenia, anxiety, depression, bipolar disorder; Hansen & Hagerman, 2003).

Indirect Assessment

Indirect assessment involves obtaining data from caregivers (e.g., parents and teachers) about the child being assessed. It has the advantage of tapping into the significant amount of experiences working with and observing the child typically possessed by caregivers. However, it is important to acknowledge the subjective nature of indirect assessment. On some occasions caregivers have biased and/or inaccurate views of a child's behavior (Goin & Myers, 2004). Thus, direct assessment (to be discussed next) is also an important element of any diagnostic assessment. From the author's experiences, the following rating scales and interview are offered as potentially valuable tools for use by the mental health professional who is attempting to diagnose autism.

Rating scales. The *Gilliam Autism Rating Scale—Second Edition* (GARS-2; Gilliam, 2005) is a behavioral checklist designed to assist in the diagnosis of autism among individuals 3 through 22 years of age. It consists of 42 items grouped into three subscales (i.e., Stereotyped Behaviors, Communication, and Social Interaction). A structured parent interview form replaces the Early Development subscale found on the original *GARS* (Gilliam, 1995). Items are based definitions of autism adopted by the American Psychiatric Association and the Autism Society of America. According to *GARS-2* marketing materials, this measure's validity has been documented by demonstrating that its standard scores discriminate persons with autism from those with severe behavior disorders such as multi-disabilities and mental retardation.

Designed to be completed by a parent, teacher, or other caregiver who knows the individual well [i.e., someone who has "... had regular, sustained contact with the subject for at least 2 weeks" (Gilliam, 1995, p. 9)], no special training is required to administer or score the *GARS*, and it is suggested most raters will be able to complete it in 5 to 10 minutes.

GARS subtest raw scores are converted into standard scores, which are then summed and in turn converted to an Autism Index (AI). For examiners using the original *GARS* (Gilliam, 1995), subtest standard scores of 8 and above and AIs (previously referred to as the "Autism Quotient") of 90 and above are associated with "Average" and above probabilities of the subject being a person with autism. Conversely, subtest standard scores below 8 and AIs below 90 are associated with "Below Average" probabilities of autism. However, when using the original version of the *GARS*, it is important to keep in mind research suggesting that the *GARS* underestimates the likelihood of autism. In a study by South and colleagues (2002), the mean *GARS* AQ of a sample composed of children already diagnosed by expert clinicians with autism was significantly lower than the reference mean. While the *GARS* mean is 100, the mean in this sample of 119 children with strict *DSM IV* (APA, 1994) diagnoses of autism was 90.10. Given its high false negative rate (52 percent in the South et al. study), the *GARS* would not appear to be appropriate for use as a screening tool. Diagnosticians using this tool should take into account that its scores may underestimate the likelihood of autism and the results of this (or any rating scale) should never be used as the sole criteria for making a diagnosis.

The *Asperger Syndrome Diagnostic Scale* (ASDS; Myles, Bock, & Simpson, 2001) is a behavioral checklist designed to assist in the diagnosis of Asperger's Disorder among individuals 5 through 18 years of age. Its 50 items are divided among five subtests (i.e., Language, Social, Maladaptive, Cognitive, and Sensorimotor) and are scored on a 2-point scale (with "0" corresponding to "Not Observed" and "1" corresponding to "Observed"). It is intended to be completed by a parent, teacher, or other caregiver who knows the individual well [i.e., someone who has "... had regular, sustained contact with the examinee for at least 2 weeks" (Myles et al., 2001, p. 9)]. Beyond having familiarity with autism, no special training is required to administer or score this measure, and it is suggested most raters will be able to complete all subtests in 10 to 15 minutes.

Subtest raw scores are converted into standard scores, which are then summed and in turn converted to an Asperger Syndrome Quotient (ASQ). It is this score, the ASQ, which is recommended for use in helping to diagnose Asperger's Disorder. Subtest standard scores are not recommended for this use. ASQs of 90 and above are associated with "Likely" to "Very Likely" probabilities of the child being a person with an Asperger's Disorder (the higher the score the greater the probability). Conversely, ASQs below 80 are associated with an "Unlikely" probability of this disorder.

The *ASDS* is considered to be psychometrically sound (Mirenda, 2003). It has been suggested to have "moderate to good reliability estimates." However, some questions have been raised about the construction of the standardization sample (i.e., there apparently was no confirmation of the Asperger's Disorder diagnoses; Blair, 2003).

The *Pervasive Developmental Disorders Screening Test–II* (PDDST-II; Siegel, 2004) is another indirect assessment tool useful in the diagnosis of autism. As was mentioned in Chapter 4, this measure has three stages, with the *PDDST-II: Stage 3* intended for use within an autism specialty clinic. Designed to discriminate children with Autistic Disorder from other PDDs, if eight or more of the *Stage 3* items are checked as being "YES, Usually True," then the result is considered a positive finding for Autistic Disorder and not another autism spectrum disorder. A valuable diagnostic addition to the *PDDST-II* is the 41-item reproducible supplemental questionnaire included in this measure's manual. This questionnaire can be used to gain additional information from parents and may prove helpful in identifying other disorders related to autism that may require additional assessment. Preliminary psychometric data was obtained by studying the *PDDST-II: Stage 3's* ability to delineate 355 children with Autistic Disorder from 99 children with another autism spectrum disorder (i.e., PDD-NOS, Asperger's Disorder). Results of this study suggested that the *PDDST–II: Stage 3* has a sensitivity of .58 and specificity of .60 (Siegel, 2004).

Interview. Developed by Rutter, Le Couteur, and Lord (2003), the *Autism Diagnostic Interview—Revised* (ADI-R) represents one of the more recently published tools for use in the diagnosis of autism. Along with the *Autism Diagnostic Observation Schedule* (ADOS), the *ADI-R* is currently considered the "gold standard" for the diagnosis of autism (Filipek et al., 1999, p. 459). According to Klinger and Renner (2000): "The diagnostic interview that yields the most reliable and valid diagnosis of autism is the *ADI–R*" (p. 481).

The *ADI-R* employs a semistructured interview format to elicit the information needed to diagnose autism. It provides separate algorithms for diagnosis and treatment or educational planning (with the latter referencing the full developmental history and the former focusing on current behavior). The interviews primary focus is on the three core domains of autism (i.e., language/communication; reciprocal social interactions; and restricted, repetitive, and stereotyped behaviors and interests). The *ADI-R* requires a trained interviewer and caregiver familiar with both the developmental history and the current behavior of the child. According to Rutter and colleagues (2003):

… in everyday clinical practice, the material provided in chapters 2 and 3 [of the ADI-R manual], together with the WPS set of teaching videotapes, will provide a sufficient introduction to the ADI-R for professionals who have prior training and experience in conducting extended clinical interviews and in working with individuals with ASDs. (p. 1)

In addition, it is important to note that the individual being assessed must have a developmental level of at least two years. The 93 items that compose this measure take approximately 90 to 150 minutes to administer. This lengthy administration time represents one of the primary limitations of this tool. In addition, it is important to reiterate that, as with all indirect assessments, the *ADI-R* is influenced by parental perceptions and agendas (Klinger & Renner, 2000).

Examination of the *ADI-R* manual suggests that it has solid psychometric properties (Rutter et al., 2003). The authors conclude that "... the *ADI-R* works very well for differentiation of ASD from nonautistic developmental disorders in clinically referred groups, provided that the mental age is above 2 years, 0 months" (p. 47). Among the *ADI-R's* domains of autistic behavior and diagnosis, interrater reliability and retest reliability have been described as "consistently convincing" (Hill et al., 2001, p. 187). Autism false positives are very rare, even when being used to differentially diagnose children with language disorders from those with high-functioning autism (Mildenberger, Sitter, Noterdaeme, & Amorosa, 2001; Noterdaeme, Mildenberger, Sitter, & Amorosa, 2002). The *ADI-R* algorithm is also reported to work well for the identification of Asperger's Disorder. However, it may not do so as well among children under 4 years of age.

Direct Assessment

Direct assessment involves obtaining data by observing the child suspected to have autism. It has the advantage of being relatively objective and is not as easily influenced by biased and/or inaccurate caregiver perceptions of the child's behavior. However, it is important to acknowledge that the behavior of children with autism can be quite variable (from one situation to the next), thus the generalizability of this type of assessment data must always be questioned. Consequently, the indirect assessments just discussed are also important elements of any diagnostic assessment. By questioning caregivers about the behaviors observed during a direct assessment, the examiner will be able to determine if the obtained observational data is typical. Based on the experiences of the authors, the following direct assessment techniques are offered as potentially valuable tools for use by the school psychologist who is attempting to diagnose autism.

Autism Diagnostic Observation Schedule (ADOS). As was just mentioned, the *ADOS* (Lord, Rutter, DiLavore, & Risi, 1999a, 1999b) is considered to be part of the "gold standard" in the diagnosis of autism (Filipek et al., 1999, p. 460). The *ADOS* is a standardized, semistructured interactive play assessment of social behavior. By making use of "planned social occasions" the *ADOS* facilitates observation of the social, communication, and play or imaginative use of material behaviors related to the diagnosis of autism.

The *ADOS* consists of four modules. Module 1 is designed for individuals who are preverbal or who speak in single words, Module 2 for those who speak in phrases, Module 3 for children and adolescents with fluent speech, and Module 4 for adolescents and adults with fluent speech. Administration of the *ADOS* requires 30 to 45 minutes and provides social-communication sequences that involve "presses" for particular social behaviors. Because its primary goal is accurate diagnosis, the authors suggest that it may not be a good measure of treatment effectiveness or developmental growth (especially in the later modules).

Psychometric data for a limited sample ($n = 223$) of disabled children and adults with and without autism is presented. "Substantial" interrater and test-retest reliability for individual items, "excellent" interrater reliability within *ADOS* domains, and internal consistency are reported (Lord et al., 2000, p. 205). Mean test scores were found to consistently differentiate autism and non-autism groups. The *ADOS* (in combination with the *ADI-R*) was found to be useful in the differential diagnosis of children with high-functioning autism from those with a receptive language disorder (Noterdaeme et al., 2002). However, the *ADOS* was less consistently able to differentiate among the autism spectrum disorders (Klinger & Renner, 2000).

Childhood Autism Rating Scale (CARS). At one time considered to be the "strongest" objective scale for the diagnosis of autism (Morgan, 1988), the *CARS* (Schopler, Reichler, & Renner, 1988) is one of the most widely used diagnostic tools for children over 2 years of age (Young & Brewer, 2002). The *CARS* is a 15-item structured observation tool. Each *CARS* item is scored on a 4-point scale ranging from 1 (normal) to 4 (severely abnormal). In making these ratings, the evaluator is asked to compare the child being assessed to others of the same developmental level. Thus, an understanding of developmental expectations for the 15 *CARS* items is essential.

The sum of the *CARS* ratings is used to determine a total score and the severity of autistic behaviors (i.e., non-autistic, 15 to 29; mildly-moderately autistic; 30 to 37; severely autistic, 37+). In addition to direct observation of the child, *CARS* data can be obtained from parent interviews and student record reviews. The author's (Brock) use of this tool involved discussion of each *CARS* item by the entire assessment team during a case staffing. In this way, it reflected the observations of several different evaluators (e.g., the language specialist, special education teacher, and school psychologist).

When the *CARS* was developed, it attempted to include diagnostic criteria from a variety of classification systems and different theoretical perspectives, and it offers no weighting of the 15 scales when determining the total score. This may have created some problems for its current use given that the field of autism study has begun to move toward consensus regarding the primary symptoms of these disorders. As a result, the *CARS* currently includes items that are no longer considered essential for the diagnosis of autism (e.g., taste, smell, and touch response) and may imply to some users of this tool that they are essential to diagnosis (when in fact they are not; Prizant, 1992). In addition, it is important to acknowledge that the *CARS* has a tendency to incorrectly classify non-autistic children with mental retardation as autistic (Deisinger, 2001).

Psychometrically, the *CARS* has been described as "acceptable" (Prizant, 1992), "good" (Young & Brewer, 2002), and as a "well-constructed rating scale" (Welsh, 1992). Validity studies have suggested that following a review of the manual and, when indicated, the viewing of a training video, the *CARS* can be used by individuals from a variety of different disciplines (including those with limited experience with autism; Prizant, 1992).

Concluding Comments

While not all school psychologists will be prepared to diagnose a specific autism spectrum disorder, it will not be surprising to find most involved in some way in the diagnostic process. This reality, combined with the fact that hearing officers often consider *DSM IV-TR* diagnostic criteria, emphasizes the importance for all educators (and, in particular, school psychologists) to be informed about diagnostic procedures.

6
Psycho-educational Assessment

Although diagnosing a specific autism spectrum disorder is not necessarily an educational responsibility, *all school psychologists should be able to conduct the psycho-educational evaluation of students with autism.* From these evaluations student strengths and challenges are identified and important program planning data obtained (including the development of specific learning goals and objectives and the documentation of possible special education eligibility). As was mentioned in Chapter 1, the *Diagnostic and Statistical Manual of Mental Disorders* [(DSM IV-TR); American Psychiatric Association (APA), 2000] diagnostic criteria are not synonymous with *Individuals with Disabilities Education Improvement Act* (IDEIA) eligibility criteria. Although suggestive of the need for supportive services, a specific autism diagnosis is not sufficient when determining special education eligibility. Thus, school psychologists will need to conduct assessments to assist IEP teams in determining if a student with autism requires special education assistance.

When assessing the developmental levels (or present levels of functioning) of students with autism, it is essential to keep in mind that the core deficits of these disorders can significantly impact test performance (Goodlin-Jones & Solomon, 2003; Shriver, Allen, & Mathews, 1999). For example, as pointed out by Loftin & Lantz (2003), the student's qualitative impairments in communication may make it difficult for him or her to respond to verbal test items (especially those that involve multiple steps) and/or generate difficulty understanding the directions that accompany many nonverbal tests. In addition, qualitative impairments in social relations may result in difficulty establishing the joint attention necessary to complete many traditional psycho-educational tests. As a consequence of the challenges to assessment presented by autism symptoms, these students are often labeled as "untestable." Such a perception of the student with autism typically reflects a lack of knowledge of appropriate testing accommodations and modifications and specific assessment techniques (Goodlin-Jones & Solomon, 2003; Loftin & Lantz, 2003). *Thus, the ability to conduct psycho-educational assessments will require knowledge of (a) the accommodations necessary to obtain valid test results for students with autism and (b) specific assessments appropriate for use with this population.* To address these psycho-educational assessment issues, this chapter begins with an examination of autism testing accommodations and modifications, and then discusses specific psychoeducational assessment practices for use with students with autism.

Testing Accommodations and Modifications

Testing students with autism requires special expertise, training, and experience to minimize the effects of autistic behavior on test validity (Koegel, Koegel, & Smith, 1997; Siegel, Minshew, & Goldstein, 1996). The school psychologist must constantly assess the degree to which tests being used reflect symptoms of autism or the specific targeted abilities (e.g., intelligence, achievement, psychological processes). For example, in the case of an IQ test (especially one with an emphasis on verbal abilities), examiners must constantly question whether obtained scores reflect cognitive potential or the qualitative impairments in communication that are typical of autism. To address these challenges, examiners will often need to make testing accommodations (Brock, 2004). Before offering specific suggestions that might be appropriate for students with autism, it is important to acknowledge that this population is very heterogeneous (Loftin & Lantz, 2003). Thus, there is no single set of accommodations that will work for every student. Rather, it is important to consider each student as an individual and to select specific accommodations to meet specific needs. With this preface in mind, the following accommodations that might be helpful when testing the student with autism are offered.

Prepare the Student for the Testing Experience

Many students with autism have great difficulty adjusting to environmental changes. Consequently, the novel testing room environment may make it difficult for the student to perform at his or her best. Thus, before assessing the student with autism, it will be important to familiarize him or her with the examiner, the testing room, and the testing experience. This can be accomplished by having a few meetings with the student in the examiner's testing room before beginning any formal assessment procedure (Loftin & Lantz, 2003). One alternative for the student who is extremely resistant to leaving the familiar classroom environment is to find a way to conduct the assessment in the classroom itself. Obviously, this would need to be done at a time when classroom distractions are at a minimum.

Place the Testing Session in the Student's Daily Schedule

Students with autism also have difficulty adjusting to changes in routine. They may, for example, react with great distress if an expected activity does not occur at an expected time. Consequently, it is not unusual for testing sessions (which occur infrequently) to be a distressing disruption to the student's routine. Given this possibility, once the student has become familiar and comfortable with the testing environment, the next important consideration is to make sure he or she knows exactly when the testing session(s) will take place. If the student is making use of a daily and/or weekly schedule, the testing session can be placed on it, giving the student the warning he or she needs that a session will take place (Reese, Richman, Zarcone, & Zarcone, 2003). Another way to minimize disruption to the student's daily routine is to break testing sessions into smaller, more discrete segments. Doing so will also allow the student to adapt to the relatively novel testing procedures (Cummings, 2004).

Minimize Distraction

Some students with autism have unusual visual and auditory sensitivities. They may for example find certain sounds (e.g., a phone ringing, a pencil being sharpened, someone coughing) extremely distressing. Thus, before assessing the student, it will be important to inquire about such sensitivities and to make appropriate environmental adjustments. In general, it would be a good idea to minimize all distractions (Loftin & Lantz, 2003).

Make Use of Preestablished Physical Structures and Work Systems

In addition to making use of a daily schedule, another way to minimize the disruption to routine is to place the session within a preestablished physical structure and work system. For example, in a classroom that makes use of structured teaching techniques (e.g., Mesibov, Shea, & Schopler, 2005; Schopler, Reichler, & Lansing, 1980), testing could take place in the preestablished one-on-one work area and make use of an already developed individual work system. Such systems inform students how much testing will be done (for example, by placing selected test items in "to do" baskets), indicates when a testing item is completed (for example, by placing test materials in a "finished basket"), and specifies what will happen once testing is completed (Marcus, Flagler, & Robinson, 2001; Marcus, Lansing, & Schopler, 1993). As will be discussed next, this last element can help to facilitate the use of external motivation for engaging in testing.

Make Use of Powerful External Rewards

Given the just mentioned challenges (i.e., sensory issues and difficulty adjusting to changes in environment and routine), it will not be surprising to find students with autism unmotivated to perform in testing sessions. In fact, they may find it aversive. Thus, it will be important to consider how to reward test performance and increase test-taking motivation (Goodlin-Jones & Solomon, 2003). Specific strategies include the use of frequent reinforcement breaks (Koegel et al., 1997) and behavioral shaping (Siegel et al., 1996). One way to inform the student of pending reinforcement breaks is to place a desired task on the student's daily schedule immediately after the testing session. In this way, the student will be informed that once testing is completed (e.g., all test materials are in the "finished basket"), a desirable activity will immediately follow (Marcus et al. 2001; Marcus et al., 1993). Using this strategy it may be possible to classically condition positive feelings about test taking. The specific rewards selected may make use of some of the unusual and intense interests held by students with autism (Reese et al., 2003). For example, at the conclusion of testing the student may be allowed to count cars as they pass by the classroom window or review baseball statistics. Of course, as is the case with all efforts to use external rewards to influence behavior, it will be essential to ensure that the individual student finds the selected reinforcer reinforcing. In addition, parents and/or teachers should always be consulted about the appropriateness of the selected reinforcers.

Carefully Preselect Task Difficulty

Another strategy to maintain the student's motivation is to alternate difficult tasks (typically language items) with easy tasks (e.g., visual problem-solving tasks; Loftin & Lantz, 2003; Marcus et al. 2001; Marcus et al., 1993). Data obtained from classroom observations and parent and teacher interviews should inform the examiner regarding what kinds of tasks will be difficult for the student and what tasks will be easy. With this knowledge, difficult tasks can be followed by what is expected to be an easy task, which can help to maintain the student's test taking motivation.

Modify Test Administration and Allow Nonstandard Responses

Many of the just mentioned accommodations might be implemented without having to break standardized test administration and scoring procedures. Obviously, to the extent it is possible, standardized administrations are preferred. However, if it becomes necessary, changing test directions (e.g., simplifying, shortening, and/or repeating them), allowing the student to respond to the task in alternative ways (e.g., using a picture communication system), and/or allowing additional time to respond to test items would be appropriate (Marcus et al., 2001; Marcus et al., 1993). Although such administrations will affect the examiner's ability to compare the student's test performance to those of students in the given standardization sample, such non-standard administrations can be very helpful in understanding the student's relative pattern of strengths and weaknesses.

Specific Psycho-educational Assessment Practices

In addition to knowledge of appropriate testing accommodations and modifications, it is also essential that the school psychologist be knowledgeable of the specific assessment practices and tools often useful when assessing the student with autism. Thus, this section will provide a review of behavioral observation and functional assessment and specific psycho-educational tests (i.e., tests of cognitive functioning, adaptive behavior, language functioning, perceptual processing, academic/developmental functioning, and emotional functioning). Developmental, health, and family history should also be a part of the comprehensive psycho-educational evaluation, and for information about the important elements of this assessment practice, the reader is referred to the discussion of this topic in Chapter 5.

Behavioral Observations and Functional Assessment

As is the case with all psycho-educational assessments, behavioral observations are essential. Students with autism are a very heterogeneous group, and in addition to the core features of autism, it is not unusual for them to display a range of behavioral symptoms including hyperactivity, short attention span, impulsivity, aggressiveness, self-injurious behavior, and (particularly in young children) temper tantrums (Hendren, 2003). Obviously, identification of these unique behavioral challenges will be important for educational program planning.

Observation of the student with autism in typical environments, such as the classroom, will also facilitate the evaluation of test taking behavior. From such observations, judgments regarding how typical the student's test taking behaviors were can be made and the validity of the obtained test results assessed. In addition to being used to assess the validity of test results, observing the student's test taking behavior may also help to document the core features of autism. For example, observation of communication abilities, eye contact with the examiner, and parent and/or teacher separation and reunification behaviors are among the behaviors that might be documented during the testing session (Siegel, 1996).

Parent and teacher interviews will also be important to understanding the student's behavior and are key elements of a functional behavioral assessment. O'Neill and colleagues (1997) provide recommendations for conducting such interviews. From the work of O'Neill and his colleagues, Figure 6.1 provides the author's (Brock) functional assessment interview form. From research conducted by Reese and colleagues (2003), it is suggested that during these interviews special attention be directed toward disruptive behaviors that gain access to perseverative behaviors and/or escape demands while engaging in these behaviors.

Psycho-educational Testing

Although specialized tests are necessary to diagnoses an autism spectrum disorder, when administered with the previously mentioned accommodations and modifications in mind, a variety of traditional psycho-educational measures are appropriate when determining the student with autism's present levels of function. From the authors' applied experiences and a review of the literature, the following measures are suggested to be possibilities for inclusion in the psycho-educational evaluation of students with autism.

Functional Assessment of Behavior

Student: _____   Age _____   Gender: _____
Date of interview: _____ Interviewer: _____ Interviewee: _____

Target Behavior(s):

_____
_____
_____
_____
_____

Behavior History:
How long have the target behavior(s) been a problem? _____
_____
_____

What has previously been tried to address the target behavior? _____
_____
_____
_____

What has been the effect of the previous behavior? _____
_____
_____
_____

Consequences of the Target Behavior(s):
What happens immediately after the behavior(s) that might be reinforcing? _____
_____
_____
_____

What does the student get? _____
_____
_____

What does the student avoid? _____
_____
_____

Are there specific/unique situations that typically generate specific consequences? If so what are those situations? _____
_____
_____

Replacement Behavior(s):
What other behavior(s), which are incompatible with the target behavior(s) and ideally obtain the same goals as target behavior, can be encouraged? Define the replacement behavior(s) in terms that are measurable and readily observable. _____
_____
_____
_____

Does the student currently display this behavior(s), or does it need to be taught to the student? _____
_____

FIGURE 6.1. This figure provides an interview form appropriate for use when collecting behavioral data.

Consequences of the Replacement Behavior(s) [S_{RF}]:
*What happens immediately after the behavior(s) that might be reinforcing?*_____
_____
_____
_____

*What does the student get?*_____
_____
_____

*What does the student avoid?*_____
_____
_____

*Are there specific/unique situations that typically generate specific consequences? If so what are those situations?*_____
_____
_____

Establishing Operations
What events, when present, make it more or less likely that the target or replacement behaviors be viewed as reinforcing and are thus more likely to occur?

a) *What medications is the student taking?* _____
_____
   What effect do they have on the target behavior? _____
_____
   What effect to they have on the replacement behavior? _____
_____

b) *Does the student have any medical or physical conditions (e.g., asthma, allergies, rashes, dental problems, sinus infections, seizures, etc.)?*_____
_____
   What effect do they have on the target behavior? _____
_____
   What effect to they have on the replacement behavior? _____
_____

c) *What are the student's sleep patterns?* _____
_____
   What effect do they have on the target behavior? _____
_____
   What effect to they have on the replacement behavior? _____
_____

d) *What are the student's eating patterns or diet?* _____
   What effect do they have on the target behavior? _____
_____
   What effect to they have on the replacement behavior? _____
_____

FIGURE 6.1. *Continued*

e)   *How predictable is the student's daily routine?* _____

What effect does the routine have on the target behavior? _____

What effect does the routine have on the replacement behavior? _____

f)   *What are some of the choices the student may be able to make during the course of a school day?*
What effect does the ability to make choices have on the target behavior? _____

What effect does the ability to make choices have on the replacement behavior? _____

g)   *Are there some situations, settings, or days that present the student with an unusually crowded
and/or noisy environment?* _____
What effect does a crowded or noisy environment have on the target behavior? _____

What effect does a crowded or noisy environment have on there placement behavior? _____

h)   *What is the pattern of staffing support present in the student's environment (e.g., 1:1 or 2:1)?* ____

Is there a particular staffing level that has an effect on the target and/or replacement behavior? _____

*Are their types of staff interactions that appear to have an effect on the target and/or replacement
behavior?* _____

Does the type of staff training have an effect on the target and/or replacement behavior? _____

i)   *Are there any other events, occurring either the night before, or the morning that, the behavior
was displayed, that are suspected to play a role in the target and/or replacement behaviors?* ____

Immediate Antecedents [S^D]:
*What are the specific events that immediately precede/predict the target and replacement behaviors?
These events are the cues, signals, or signposts that tell the student that a given behavior will yield a
reinforcing outcome.*

a)   **Time of day.**
When is the target behavior most likely to occur? _____
When is the replacement behavior most likely to occur? _____
When is the target behavior least likely to occur? _____
When is the replacement behavior least likely to occur? _____
b)   **Setting.**
Where is the target behavior most likely to occur? _____
Where is the replacement behavior most likely to occur? _____
Where is the target behavior least likely to occur? _____
Where is the replacement behavior least likely to occur? _____
c)   **People.**
With whom is the target behavior most likely to occur? _____
With whom is the replacement behavior most likely to occur? _____
With whom is the target behavior least likely to occur? _____
With whom is the replacement behavior least likely to occur? _____

FIGURE 6.1. *Continued*

d)   **Activity**.
During what activities is the target behavior most likely to occur? _____
During what activities is the replacement behavior most likely to occur? _____
During what activities is the target behavior least likely to occur? _____
During what activities is the replacement behavior least likely to occur? _____

e)   **Other antecedents**.
Are there any other antecedents that appear to cue or trigger the target behavior (e.g., specific task demands, noises, lights, clothes, smells, etc.)? _____
_____

f)   *If you wanted to guarantee that the target behavior would occur, what would you do?* _____
_____
_____
_____
_____
_____
_____
_____
_____

Summary Statements: EO[(S^D)R>S$_{RE}$)]

Antecedents		Target Behavior	Consequences
EO *Distant Setting Event*	*S^D* *Immediate Antecedent* *(Trigger)*	*R* *Response*	*S$_{RF}$* *Rewarding Stimulus*

Antecedents		Target Behavior	Consequences
EO *Distant Setting Event*	*S^D* *Immediate Antecedent* *(Trigger)*	*R* *Response*	*S$_{RF}$* *Rewarding Stimulus*

Antecedents		Target Behavior	Consequences
EO *Distant Setting Event*	*S^D* *Immediate Antecedent* *(Trigger)*	*R* *Response*	*S$_{RF}$* *Rewarding Stimulus*

FIGURE 6.1. *Continued*

Cognitive functioning. Assessment of cognitive function is essential given that, with the exception of Asperger's Disorder, a significant percentage of students with autism will also be mentally retarded (APA, 2000; Chakrabarti & Fombonne, 2001; Ritvo et al., 1989; Volkmar & Cohen, 1986; Young & Brewer, 2002). The presence of mental retardation also has diagnostic implications as *DSM IV-TR* (APA, 2000) specifies that the presence of severe to profound retardation will make it difficult to diagnose Autistic Disorder.

In addition, to ruling in or ruling out mental retardation, the student's level of cognitive functioning provides data important to educational program planning (Tidmarsh & Volkmar, 2003). For example, IQ is associated with adaptive functioning, the ability to learn and acquire new skills, and long-term prognosis. Thus, level of cognitive functioning has significant implications for determining how restrictive the educational environment will need to be. IQ test results can also be helpful in differential diagnosis among the various autism spectrum disorders. Specifically, students with Rett's Disorder typically have profound to severe IQ deficits, those with Childhood Disintegrative Disorder typically have severe deficits, those with Autistic Disorder typically have moderate deficits, and those with Asperger's Disorder do not typically have any cognitive delay (APA, 2000). IQ testing has even been suggested to distinguish among individuals with Asperger's Disorder and high-functioning autism. In a recent study, individuals with Asperger's Disorder obtained higher verbal IQs and higher scores on information and vocabulary subtests when compared with those with high-functioning autism (Ghaziuddin & Mountain-Kimchi, 2004).

Intelligence test performance is also a powerful predictor of autism symptom severity, with higher IQ scores being associated with less severe autism symptoms (Filipek et al., 1999; Goodlin-Jones & Solomon, 2003). However, given that children with autism are ideally first evaluated when they are very young (i.e., 2 to 3 years of age), it is important to keep in mind that it is not until age 5 that childhood IQ correlates highly with adult IQ (Sattler, 1988). In addition, the anecdotal observations of Goodlin-Jones and Solomon (2003) suggest that

... developmental quotients of very young children with autism, especially those who had normal early motor development (suggesting less neurodevelopmental dysfunction), are generally not predictive of response to treatment and potential for growth. That is, many children who do poorly on tests will still improve significantly with intervention. (p. 71)

Similarly, Marcus and colleagues (1993) suggest, "with the preschooler...such prognostic indicators [IQ testing] should either not be used or used only with considerable caution" (p. 329). Thus, it is important to treat the IQ scores of the very young child with caution when offering a prognosis and when making placement and program planning decisions. However, for school-aged children it is clear that the appropriate IQ test is an "excellent predictor of a student's later adjustment and functioning in real life" (Frith, 1989, p. 84). Filipek and colleagues (1999) suggest that it may be beneficial to conduct IQ testing before kindergarten entry to help with curriculum planning. In addition, such IQ test results can provide a baseline and serve as one way to measure intervention effectiveness.

Regardless of the overall level of cognitive functioning, it is not unusual for the student being tested to display an uneven profile of cognitive abilities (Lincoln, Allen, & Kilman, 1995). Especially during the preschool years, among students with Autistic Disorder, verbal IQs tend to lag behind non-verbal IQs (although this gap is not expected to be as large among those assessed during their school-age

TABLE 6.1. IQ test appropriate for use with students who have spoken language.

Intelligence test	Age range
Wechsler Preschool and Primary Scale of Intelligence, Third Edition (Wechsler, 2002)	3–7 years
Wechsler Intelligence Scale for Children, Fourth Edition (Wechsler, 2003)	6–16 years
Wechsler Adult Intelligence Scale, Third Edition (Wechsler, 1997)	16 years and up
Wechsler Abbreviated Scale of Intelligence (Wechsler, 1999)	6–89 years
Stanford-Binet Intelligence Scale, Fifth Edition (Roid, 2003)	2 years to adult
Differential Ability Scales (Elliott, 1990)	2–17 years

years; Mayes & Calhoun, 2003). Thus, rather than simply providing an overall global intelligence test score, it is essential to identify these cognitive strengths and weaknesses. Doing so will assist educational planning (Filipek et al., 1999). At the same time, however, it is important to avoid the temptation to generalize from isolated or "splinter" skills when forming an overall impression of cognitive functioning, given that such skills may significantly overestimate typical abilities (National Research Council, 2001).

Selection of specific tests is important to obtaining a valid assessment of cognitive functioning (and not the symptoms characteristic of autism). Goodlin-Jones and Solomon (2003) suggest that the *Wechsler* (2003) and *Stanford-Binet* (Roid, 2003) scales are appropriate for the individual with spoken language. On the other hand, for students who have more severe language delays, measures that minimize verbal demands are recommended. Goodlin-Jones and Solomon suggest that the *Leiter International Performance Scale*, Revised (Roid & Miller, 1997) "is a reasonable choice for assessing a child who has limited language ability or is nonverbal" (p. 68). Adapted from Cummings (2004), Tables 6.1 and 6.2 provide listings of tests for use in assessing students with autism who have language abilities and those who have communication challenges.

Adaptive behavior. As was just mentioned, the majority of individuals with autism also have mental retardation. Given that diagnosing mental retardation requires

TABLE 6.2. IQ test appropriate for use with students who have communication challenges.

Intelligence test	Age range
Leiter International Performance Scales, Revised (Roid & Miller, 1997)	2–21 years
Bayley Scales of Infant Development–II (Bayley, 1993)	1–42 months
Mullen Scales of Early Learning (Mullen, 1995)	1–60 months
Columbia Mental Maturity Scale, Third Edition (Burgemeister, Blum, & Lorge, 1972)	3.5–10 years
Raven's Coloured Progressive Matrices (Raven, Court & Raven, 1986; cited in Deisinger, 2001)	5–11 years
Test of Nonverbal Intelligence, Third Edition (Brown, Sherbenou, & Johnsen, 1997)	5 years and up
Kaufman Assessment Battery for Children, Second Edition (Kaufman & Kaufman, 2004)	2–12 years

examination of both IQ and adaptive behavior (APA, 2000), it is also important to administer measures of adaptive behavior when assessing students with autism (Klin, Carter, & Sparrow, 1997). According to Carter and colleagues (1998), other uses of adaptive behavior scales when assessing students with autism are (1) identifying strengths and weaknesses for educational planning and intervention, (2) documenting intervention efficacy, and (3) monitoring progress over time. Regarding this last purpose, it is important to note that children with autism have been shown to improve in all adaptive behavior domains (as measured by the *Vineland Adaptive Behavior Scales*; Sparrow, Balla, & Cicchetti, 1984) over time. However, the rate of growth in the Communication and Daily Living Skills domains is related to initial IQ. The rate of growth in the Social Skills domain is independent of initial IQ (Freeman, Del'Homme, Guthrie, & Zhang, 1999).

When interpreting the results of these scales, it is important to keep in mind that the profiles of students with autism are unique. While individuals with only mental retardation typically display flat profiles across adaptive behavior domains, students with autism might be expected to display relative strengths in daily living skills, relative weaknesses in socialization skills, and intermediate scores on measures of communication abilities (Bölte & Poustka, 2002; Carter et al., 1998).

Language functioning. A speech and language pathologist should conduct a comprehensive examination of language functioning whenever a student with autism is being considered for special education services. However, there may be instances where the school psychologist needs to obtain estimates of expressive and receptive language, and Goodlin-Jones and Solomon (2003) recommend the *Peabody Picture Vocabulary Test*, Third Edition (Dunn & Dunn, 1997) and the *Expressive One-Word Picture Vocabulary Test* (Brownell, 2000) for such use. When interpreting the results of these measures, it is important to keep in mind that these tests may overestimate language abilities as they do not require sentence production or comprehension, nor do they assess social language or pragmatics (Goodlin-Jones & Solomon, 2003). In addition, among many higher functioning students with autism, receptive language abilities may be lower than expressive language skill (APA, 2000).

Psychological processes. The comprehensive psycho-educational evaluation of the student with autism will also require the school psychologist to evaluate basic psychological processes. Doing so will help to further identify learning strengths and weaknesses important to program planning. In addition, it is possible that the student may have a comorbid learning disability that will require special education intervention in its own right. Depending upon the student's age and developmental level, traditional measures of such processes may be appropriate.

It would not be surprising to find the student with autism to exhibit spared rote, mechanical, and visual-spatial processes; and deficient higher-order conceptual processes, such as abstract reasoning (Ehlers et al., 1997; Goodlin-Jones & Solomon, 2003). Visual reasoning might also be expected to be relatively high when compared with measures of graphomotor skill (Mayes & Calhoun, 2003).

Although IQ test profiles should never be used for diagnostic purposes, it would not be surprising to find the student with Autistic Disorder to perform better on non-verbal (visual/spatial) tasks (in particular the *WISC* Block Design subtest) and poorer on tasks that require verbal comprehension and expression (Ehlers et al., 1997; Siegel et al., 1996). The student with Asperger's Disorder may display the opposite profile (Goodlin-Jones & Solomon, 2003), with lower scores on Object Assembly and Coding subsets (Ehlers et al., 1997). In addition, in comparison with Autistic Disorder, students with Asperger's Disorder might be expected to have relatively well developed crystallized abilities. Students with Autistic Disorder typically perform poorly on acquired knowledge tasks (Ehlers et al., 1997).

Although attention problems are often noted among students with autism, they are not of the type typically seen among those with Attention-deficit/Hyperactivity Disorder (AD/HD). Whereas students with ADHD typically have more difficulty with sustained attention and are more distracted by external environmental stimuli, those with autism are typically more distracted by internal factors, such as their own special and intense interests (Garretson, Fein, & Waterhouse, 1990). Students with autism are also more likely to overfocus attention on irrelevant details while missing the main ideas. However, ADHD can coexist with autism (Goodlin-Jones & Solomon, 2003). If comorbid ADHD is suspected, then it is recommended that an ADHD evaluation be conducted using methods such as those described by Brock (1999).

Academic/developmental functioning. A special-education teacher should conduct a comprehensive examination of academic functioning. However, there may be instances where school psychologists need to obtain estimates of achievement. As was the case for cognitive assessment, assessment of academic functioning will often reveal a profile of strengths and weaknesses important to educational planning. Variability among achievement test scores is common. For example, it is not unusual for students with autism to be hyperverbal and hyperlexic while at the same time having poor reading comprehension and difficulties dealing with abstract language. For other students, calculation skills may be well developed, while mathematical concepts may be delayed (Marcus et al., 2001). Among students classified as high-functioning autistic, it would not be surprising to find writing skills a relative weakness, whereas among those with low IQ scores reading may be a relative strength (Mayes & Calhoun, 2003).

For students functioning at or below the preschool range and/or with a chronological age of 6 months to 7 years, the *Psycho-educational Profile—Third Edition* (PEP-3; Schopler, Lansing, Reichler, & Marcus, 2005) may be an appropriate choice. Recently revised, the *PEP-3* was standardized on national samples of children with autism and children who were typically developing (thus allowing for comparisons to both groups). The *PEP-3* kit now contains virtually all stimulus items which previous versions of the *PEP* required individual examiners to collect on their own. Another new element of the *PEP-3* is the inclusion of a Caregiver Report that obtains additional data regarding the student's developmental level. Like its predecessors, the *PEP-3* produces a profile that graphically charts a student's development and emerging skills in a variety of function domains. It also charts autistic behaviors. As such, it is a particularly helpful tool when it comes to program planning and IEP development. For adolescents and adults with autism who are functioning in the moderate to severe range of mental retardation the *Adolescent and Adult Psychoeducational Profile* (*AAPEP*; Mesibov, Schopler, Schaffer, & Landrus, 1988) would be an appropriate choice.

For older, higher functioning students, the *Woodcock–Johnson Tests of Achievement* (Woodcock, McGrew, & Mather, 2001) and the *Wechsler Individual Achievement Test* (Wechsler, 1992) would be appropriate tools. However, Marcus and colleagues (2001) caution that formal achievement tests alone may not provide necessary information on the overall educational functioning of the student and that "a curriculum-based evaluation might provide the most useful data for the autistic population" (p. 285).

Emotional functioning. As the student with autism matures, new symptoms and behavior that interfere with daily functioning may appear. Autism can be associated with a variety of other symptoms, and 65 percent present with symptoms of an additional psychiatric disorder such as AD/HD, oppositional defiant disorder, obsessive-compulsive disorder, and other anxiety disorders, tic disorders, affective disorders, and psychotic disorders (Hendren, 2003). Given these possibilities, it will also be important for the school psychologist to evaluate the student's emotional/behavioral status. Traditional measures such as the *Behavioral Assessment System for Children* (Reynolds, & Kamphaus, 1998) would be appropriate as a general-purpose screening tool, while more specific measures such as *The Children's Depression Inventory* (Kovacs, 1992) and the *Revised Children's Manifest Anxiety Scale* (Reynolds & Richmond, 1998) would be appropriate for assessing more specific presenting concerns.

Concluding Comments

Although not all school psychologists will be prepared to diagnose a specific autism spectrum disorder, all should be capable of conducting the psycho-educational evaluation of these students. Consequently, it is essential that school psychologists be informed of the techniques and strategies helpful in obtaining valid assessment data. With this information, learning strengths and challenges can be identified, instructional goals and objectives developed, and special education eligibility determined.

7
Treatment

As discussed in Chapters 1 and 2, autism spectrum disorders are behaviorally defined disorders of development that are thought to have multiple etiologic pathways (Hansen & Hagerman, 2003; Muhle, Trentacoste, & Rapin, 2004; Newschaffer, Fallin, & Lee, 2002; Schreibman, 2005). Many different treatment strategies have been developed to address the behavioral and learning deficits among children with autism, some purportedly addressing underlying etiologic factors, although educational approaches are currently the primary and only form of intervention documented to significantly improve outcomes. Thus, the treatments reviewed in this chapter include educational interventions that comprehensively address multiple areas of development, targeted educational interventions for specific target skills, psychopharmacologic treatments for behaviors commonly found in children with ASD that interfere with learning, and a brief summary of alternative treatments that are used by many families of children with ASD but that do not currently have sufficient scientific evidence to support their use.

Despite the broad range of abilities and deficits present among children across the autism spectrum, the National Research Council's (2001) Committee on Educational Interventions for Children with Autism recommends that children with any autistic spectrum disorder, regardless of level of severity or function, receive education services as soon as possible, and that appropriate educational goals are the same as those of other children: "personal independence and social responsibility" (p. 5). Education of children with autism was accepted as a public responsibility as part of the Education Act of All Handicapped Children in 1975, yet the resources, methods, and goals of such education vary from state to state and district to district within states. Deficits in language, nonverbal communication, cognitive abilities, and sensory processing all affect the behavior and learning of children with autism and have critical implications for specific intervention strategies. Assessment of learning strengths and weaknesses as well as behavioral challenges in children with autism (see Chapter 6) is critical for establishing appropriate educational and behavioral interventions. School professionals play a critical role in the development, monitoring, and implementation of successful intervention programs for students with autism. Children with autism generally require the services of multiple professionals, including resource specialists, speech and language pathologists, occupational and physical therapists, and the school psychologist. Thus, team leaders, often times the school psychologist, must have both team building skills as well as knowledge about empirically supported practices to share with families, teachers, and other school personnel working with students with autism.

There is a large and increasing body of research documenting the effectiveness of specific intervention strategies for children with autism in addressing deficits in language, nonverbal communication, social skills, and improving challenging behaviors that interfere with learning (Bondy & Frost, 2001; Carr, Levin, McConnachie, Carlson, Duane, & Smith, 1994; Handleman & Harris, 2001; Koegel & Koegel, 1995, 2006; Mastergeorge, Rogers, Corbett, & Solomon, 2003; NRC, 2001; Rogers, 1998; Schreibman, 2000, 2005; Schreibman & Ingersoll, 2005; Schreibman & Koegel, 2005; Siegel, 1996), although the relationship between particular techniques and long-term outcomes is still not clear. This is largely because of methodological issues (NRC, 2001). However, there is consensus regarding key characteristics of effective intervention programs. These include entry into educational services as soon as a child is suspected of having an autism spectrum disorder and provision of intensive instructional programming that should include a minimum of 25 hours a week, 12 months a year, of systematically planned and developmentally appropriate educational activity toward identified objectives. These objectives should be observable, measurable behaviors and skills that affect a child's participation in the educational setting, the community, and family life. It is critical that families are active participants in the assessment and planning process, helping to identify goals and objectives as well as learning techniques used in the educational settings to teach their children new skills (NRC, 2001). Priorities of intervention should be on functional spontaneous communication, social instruction, cognitive development, and play skills, delivered throughout the day in various settings. To the extent possible, children with autism should receive interventions in a setting with ongoing interactions with typically developing peers (NRC, 2001).

Comprehensive Treatments Focusing on Multiple Developmental Skills

Preschool. Comprehensive preschool treatment programs vary in their theoretical backgrounds as well as their delivery of services. Outcome studies of different models have demonstrated significant improvements in the development of young children, although there are few studies that have used controlled group designs to directly compare different approaches. Mastergeorge and colleages (2003) review the key elements of effective early intervention programs for children with autism and conclude that (a) programs must begin early, when risk factors are recognized; (b) programs must be intensive (25 hours or more per week, 52 weeks per year) with a low student/teacher ratio; (c) intervention must involve families in the development of priorities, goals, and treatment plans and must include family training, support, and consultation; (d) interventions must be individualized to the specific needs, strengths, and interests of each child; (e) interventions must be designed and delivered by experienced, professional interdisciplinary teams; (f) objectives should target the development of social attention, peer interaction, functional spontaneous language and appropriate toy play, and use positive behavioral approaches to decrease problem behaviors; and (g) progress should be evaluated frequently and interventions adjusted when needed

Applied behavioral analysis methodology has become established as a critical component in instructional strategies demonstrated to be effective in children with autism (Carr, et al., 1994; Koegel & Koegel, 2006; Mastergeorge et al., 2003; NRC, 2001; Schreibman, 2000, 2005), both for addressing core deficits in autism as well as other challenging associated behaviors. The use of discrete trial training strategies in young children with autism using massed trial interventions with adult-directed teaching episodes (Lovaas, 1987; McEachin, Smith, & Lovaas, 1993; Smith, Eikesth, Klevstrand, & Lovaas., 1997; Smith, Groen, & Wynn 2000), as well as more child-centered techniques in which child-initiated activities (Koegel, Koegel, & Carter, 1998; Koegel & Koegel, 2006; McGee, Morrier, & Daly, 1999; Pierce & Schreibman, 1997) lead to a consequence or reinforcer, called pivotal response training and incidental teaching, has been demonstrated to be effective in teaching new skills in children with autism, as well as changing existing behaviors. The program developed by Lovaas and colleagues has primarily been used in home-based, adult-directed intervention programs, although others have delivered similar discrete trial behavioral methods in group settings (Harris, Handleman, Arnold, & Golden 2001; McClannahan & Krantz, 2001). Pivotal response training and incidental teaching methods have also been used successfully in both in-home settings and in group settings. Pivotal response training (PRT) teaches "pivotal" communication behaviors, such as requesting, by responding to the child's communicative attempt with a prompt for a more mature level of communication and then providing an intrinsic reinforcer. Incidental teaching methods create an environment that motivates communication, by providing desirable toys, activities, etc., and then using any child-initiated communication as an opportunity to prompt for more elaborate communication. These interventions require environments that provide many opportunities for communication so that these behaviors can be shaped by repetitions. Comparative data suggests that naturalistic interventions lead to more rapid generalization of language skills than the adult-directed approach espoused by Lovaas and colleagues (Koegel & Koegel, 2006; Mastergeorge et al., 2003; Schreibman, 2005).

Developmental-pragmatic approaches that emphasize relationships, affect, and play, in addition to language and other developmental skills, have been used successfully in preschool interventions (Rogers, Hall, Osaki, Reaven, & Hervison, 2001; Greenspan & Weider, 1997; Rogers & Lewis, 1989; Rogers & DiLalla, 1991). These approaches emphasize play, child-centered control of interactions and sharing emotions with others (Prizant & Wetherby, 1998) with the primary goal of fostering pleasure in relationships and teaching that communication with others is satisfying. Another developmental approach, which uses a highly visual structure and organization of the environment and materials, is the TEACCH program

(Marcus, Schopler, & Lord, 2001; Schopler, Mesibov, & Hearsay, 1995). This program structures academic, social, and communication tasks so that what is expected and how to complete it are visually apparent through use of visual schedules (in either words or pictures) and visual cues. Teachers and parents implement similar structural supports and materials at school and at home. Parents who have learned and implemented TEACCH principles report feeling more competent and less depressed, and the continuity between school and home is helpful. TEACCH treatments lend themselves to both individual and group formats (Ozonoff, Dawson, & Partland, 2002).

Use of typically developing peers within the context of preschool programs has been shown to be an effective component of educating young children with autism. Strain, Odom, Goldstein, and colleagues have developed peer-mediated interventions that have strong empirical support for increasing social interactions in children with autism (reviewed in Mastergeorge et al., 2003). Typical peers are taught to initiate sharing, helping, giving affection and praise as a way of organizing play, first with adults and then with children with autism, initially with adult cueing using typical play materials. Both generalization and maintenance of social behaviors have been successful using peer-mediated interventions in inclusive settings (Goldstein, Kaczmarek, Pennington, & Shafer, 1992; Goldstein & Strain, 1988).

School age. Educational programs for school-age children share many of the attributes of comprehensive preschool intervention programs and utilize similar intervention strategies. Close coordination and information sharing between programs and professionals during transitions are critical. Assessment of existing skills, developing measurable and individually appropriate goals and objectives for target skills, choosing appropriate teaching techniques, monitoring progress frequently and adjusting strategies when needed are essential for effective teaching and learning for children with autism. Educational interventions for school-age students include discrete trial and naturalistic behavioral principles, environmental structure and organization described in the preschool interventions, as well as peer mediation strategies. Children with autism, regardless of functional level, can be educated in inclusive settings, although the level of resource support and accommodation will vary (Harrower & Dunlap, 2001; Koegel, Koegel, Frea, & Fredeen, 2001; Stahmer, Ingersoll, & Koegel, 2004). Some students may require an aide for parts or all of the school day in order to remain included. These aides must have training in the core deficits of children with autism, understanding of the techniques used in teaching and the specific accommodations needed for their children, and training in effective behavioral management approaches. In particular, general education teachers and aides require ongoing support from school psychologists and other school professionals with special knowledge of autism.

Although a few of the highest functioning children with autism may not be eligible for special education services, all at the very least will require that their general educational program be modified in some way, and most will qualify for special education and have an Individualized Education Program (IEP). These modifications may include visual schedules, written rules and directions, reduced workload, access to assistive technology within the classroom such as computer keyboards, and computerized communication devices. School psychologists play a critical role in providing the cognitive, adaptive, and social assessments needed to develop appropriate educational curriculum for children with autism, as well as monitoring the effectiveness of the curriculum. Often, behavioral challenges are the primary impediment to placement in less restrictive settings and meeting educational goals. Psychologists must be skilled in providing functional behavioral assessment of problem behaviors within classroom settings, designing behavioral interventions, training teachers, aides, and parents in implementation of consistent behavioral interventions, and monitoring change. Psychologists are also often involved in developing and implementing social skills groups, parent training programs, and support. For further discussion of the essential elements of functional behavioral assessment, O'Neill and colleagues (1997) is a recommended resource. For further discussion of developing and implementing social skills groups, refer to Krasny, Williams, Provencal, & Ozonoff (2003) and Ozonoff et al. (2002). To be maximally effective, all intervention programs must actively involve parents, both in identifying appropriate educational goals and objectives, as well as in implementation and generalization of skills and monitoring progress. The model intervention programs discussed in this chapter incorporate parent training as a component of implementation.

Educational Interventions for Specific Target Skills

Language function. Language functioning is the strongest predictor of outcome in autism, and it has recently been documented that 75–95 percent of children with autism can develop useful speech when provided with specific language interventions that are sufficiently intense (NRC, 2001). Discrete trial training approaches have been shown to be effective in the acquisition of language, although the use of extrinsic adult-delivered reinforcement and the rote, repetitive nature of the teaching sessions has been criticized for limited generalization to spontaneous, functional communication unless this is specifically programmed. Both pivotal response training (PRT) and incidental teaching approaches have been shown to improve language development in children with autism, as have developmental-pragmatic interventions (Koegel & Koegel, 2006; Mastergeorge et al., 2003; Schreibman, 2005), although more research is needed to document whether these are as effective as the other behavioral models.

Lack of functional communication contributes to many problematic behaviors among children with autism, and providing some method of functional communication in nonverbal children is critical. The use of picture symbols, such as the Picture Exchange Communication System (PECS), has been effective in teaching nonverbal children to initiate a picture request and persist with the communication until the partner responds (Bondy & Frost, 1994, 2002). The authors provide a manual with a step-by-step teaching process. The TEACCH model (Schopler et al., 1995) also uses pictures and printed word cards. The use of sign language in nonverbal children with autism has been less successful, perhaps because of the difficulty many children with autism have in imitating hand movements (Rogers, Bennetto, McEvoy, & Pennington, 1996), although Goldstein (2002) reviews studies that have shown the successful use of sign language in teaching communication. There is evidence that nonverbal children seem more stimulated to learn speech if they already understand symbolic communication, rather than less likely, which is a concern often voiced by parents (Mastergeorge et al., 2003). In other words, it appears that once children learn that a particular method of communicating with others is helpful in meeting their needs, they are likely to learn to use other methods of communication.

Increasing pragmatic communication among verbal children with autism, including initiation of communication, turn taking, use of gestures and body language, is a critical component of intervention. Using visual prompts to increase initiations and behavioral approaches such as PRT to increase conversational gestures and improve articulation have been effective (Koegel & Koegel, 2006; Mastergeorge et al., 2003; Schreibman, 2005). Coordinating approaches with strategies to improve social skills in general is important and frequently involve close collaboration with the speech and language pathologist (Garcia Winner, 2000).

Social skills. Interventions that specifically address social skills are important for most children with autism and can be provided in a variety of ways. Adult-directed group interventions provide a scaffolded and supported setting in which to observe and practice social skills with peers. These generally involve verbal, higher functioning children with autism and include using appropriate eye contact, body language, emotion recognition and response, perspective taking, and conversational skills. Bauminger (2002) demonstrated positive outcomes in a school-based social skills group that included home interventions with parents that were sustained to the following year, although the documentation of generalized improvement in social skills outside the program are mixed (Mastergeorge et al., 2003). Additional program descriptions are included in Krasny et al. (2003), Ozonoff et al. (2002), Gutstein and Sheely (2002), and Garcia Winner (2000).

Other adult-mediated social interventions include the use of social stories written to teach social rules and appropriate social behaviors. These can be used by teachers, therapists, and parents and have been shown to increase sharing, play, and social initiations (Koegel & Koegel, 2006; Mastergeorge et al., 2003; Schreibman, 2005). Social games, visual cueing, and video modeling are other strategies with some research to support their effectiveness in improving social skills in children with autism. The effectiveness of all these strategies improve when parents are involved and can implement techniques at home consistently (Garcia Winner, 2000, 2006; Mastergeorge et al., 2003).

Peer-mediated interventions have a large body of research supporting the effectiveness of peer play in improving social skills, reflecting the emphasis on inclusion of children with disabilities such as autism. An excellent review of programs using both trained and untrained peers is provided by Mastergeorge and colleagues

(2003), demonstrating the importance of ongoing interactions of children with autism and typically developing peers on social engagements.

Behavior problems. Disruptive behaviors must be a focus of intervention, particularly if they limit the ability of children to participate in less restrictive, more inclusive environments, instructional activities, and peer interactions. School personnel who work extensively with students (such as school psychologists) with autism and/or the teachers who serve these children must be skilled in functional behavioral assessment, which is the basis for developing effective behavior intervention programs. Assessments should be provided in the context in which they occur. Identifying and quantifying target behaviors, determining antecedent events and consequences (or functions) of the behaviors, and reinforcing more adaptive behavioral substitutes are the key components in positive behavioral approaches (for reviews see Mastergeorge et al. 2003). Functional assessment can also be used to prevent behavior problems. As was mentioned in Chapter 6, functional assessment can be a part of the psychoeducational evaluation conducted by the school psychologist as an individualized education plan is being developed. For a sample functional assessment interview form see Chapter 6.

Psychopharmacologic Interventions

School psychologists play an important role in helping to monitor the effectiveness of medication interventions on target behaviors, as well as the side effects. Medications are adjunctive therapies to educational interventions, targeted to behaviors that are not completely addressed by behavioral interventions alone. They do not address the underlying core deficits in autism. Thus, familiarity with medications being used, the provision of quantifiable behavioral observations for deciding on target behaviors as well as for pre- and post-treatment comparison, and support of communication between teachers, parents, and physicians are all critical components of the role school psychologists play in the efficacious and safe use of medications to treat children with autism. There is very little research on the long-term consequences of psychotropic medications in young children, although many medications used to treat children with autism have been investigated in terms of short-term benefits and safety.

Neuroleptics. This category of medications has long been used to treat symptoms of aggression, self-injurious behaviors, hyperactivity, stereotypies, social withdrawal, and sleep disturbances. These medications are thought to act on the dopamine and serotonin neurotransmitter systems (brain chemicals important to central nervous system functioning). However, older neuroleptics such as haloperidol and pimozide have a high frequency of serious side effects such as movement disorders. Fewer side effects have been found using newer medications of this type, called atypical neuroleptics. The Research Units of Pediatric Psychopharmacology's (RUPP) Autism Network (2002) demonstrated the efficacy of risperidone, an atypical neuroleptic, among children with autism and severe behavior problems in a double-blind, placebo-controlled study documenting improvements in irritability, stereotypies, and hyperactivity. Increased appetite with weight gain is the most common side effect, raising concerns about hyperglycemia (elevated blood sugar). Other adverse side effects included fatigue, drowsiness, dizziness, tremor, and drooling. Other medications in this category which have been shown to be effective in open label trials include olanzapine, zipradisone, and quetiapine (Bostic & King, 2005; des Portes, Hagerman, & Hendren, 2003).

Antidepressants. Disruption of serotonergic systems in children and adults with autism has been repeatedly documented, although the relationship to specific behavioral dysfunction is less clear (des Portes et al., 2003; McDougle, Naylor, Cohen, Aghajanian, Heninger, & Price,1996a). Selective serotonin reuptake inhibitors (SSRIs) are medications that been have used to treat a variety of mood disorders such as depression and anxiety and are increasingly used to treat children with autism. Medications in this category include fluvoxamine, fluoxetine, sertraline, citalopram, and paroxetine. Studies have shown decreased repetitive behaviors, less aggression and maladaptive behaviors in children (Bostic & King, 2005; McDougle, Naylor, Cohen, Volkmar, Heninger, & Price, 1996b; Steingard, Zimnitzky, DeMaso, Bauman, & Bucci, 1997). Significant side effects include behavioral activation in some children, including insomnia, hyperactivity, agitation, aggression, anxiety, and anorexia.

Psychostimulants. Although psychostimulants (methylphenidate and dextroamphetamine) have been the most studied group of psychoactive medications in children, few studies have examined their use among children with autism. However, the existing research has demonstrated their efficacy in addressing ADHD symptoms in children with autism (Handen, Johnson, & Lobetsky, 2000; Quintana, Birmaher, Stedge, Lennon, Freed, Bridge & Greenhill, 1995), although at a lower rate than children with ADHD alone (Aman & Langworthy, 2000). Side effects are similar to children with ADHD alone and include decreased appetite, stomach aches, sleep disturbance, headache, and, rarely, tics, although at higher doses some children with autism show social withdrawal and irritability (Bostic & King, 2005; Handen et al., 2000).

Alpha-adrenergic agonists. These medications (clonidine and guanfacine) have been used to treat children with ADHD and hyperarousal, although there is limited evidence of their effectiveness in children with autism. Hagerman and colleages (1995; 2000) found clonidine to be effective in treating symptoms of ADHD, aggression, and tantrums in children with fragile X syndrome, 30 percent of whom also had autism. Side effects include sedation, hypotension, and change in heart rate, which needs to be assessed with an EKG. Abrupt discontinuation of this medication can cause headaches and rebound hypertension, so when indicated it must be gradually withdrawn.

Alternative and Complementary Treatments

The increasing prevalence of autism has led to the suggestion that exposure to unknown substances in the environment may be triggering the development of autism in genetically susceptible individuals. As was discussed in Chapter 2, there is currently no conclusive data to support any specific environmental exposure or genetically identifiable subgroup with autism at increased risk for exposure to an environmental agent such as vaccines, mercury or other heavy metals, or pesticides, although the number of potentially neurotoxic agents in the environment has increased very rapidly over the past several decades.

The American Academy of Pediatrics (2001) has defined alternative and complementary treatments as "strategies that have not met the standards of clinical effectiveness, either through randomized controlled clinical trials or through the consensus of the biomedical community." Despite the lack of information on either the benefits or risks of alternative therapies, and the absence of known etiologic mechanisms in autism, many parents are choosing to use alternative and complementary approaches to treating their children with autism. Surveys suggest that 30 percent (Levy, Mandell, Nerhar, Ittenback, & Pinto-Martin, 2003) to 90 percent (Harrington, Rosen, Garnecho & Patrick, 2006) of parents of children with autism have used alternative approaches in treating their children. Parents choose these treatments for a variety of reasons, including an attempt to gain control over a disorder that is extremely disruptive to the entire family and for which there is no known cause, lack of expected progress in very labor intensive educational interventions, a concern that educational interventions are treating symptoms rather than underlying causes of autism, pressure from friends and families, anecdotal information that other children with autism have been 'cured' using these approaches, and a desire to try all possible interventions that might help their child. Unfortunately, many parents are not aware of the potential safety risks of some of these alternative interventions.

Reviews of the most common alternative treatments used by families of children with autism are provided by Hansen and Ozonoff (2003) and Levy and Hyman (2005), along with summaries of underlying theoretical mechanisms, documentation of efficacy, and potential risks. A brief summary is provided here. In general, few well-designed studies exist that have investigated the anecdotal testimonials of cures or substantial improvements found on the Internet. Most studies available are open label trials in which either or both the patient/parent and investigator know who is receiving the intervention, and most have not found positive effects when controlled for other variables.

Treatments purported to alter neurotransmitter release or production include the use of precursors of neurotransmitters such as dimethlyglycine or trimethlyglycine (DMG/TMG), vitamin B6 and magnesium, vitamin C, omega 3 fatty acids, secretin, tryptophan, and cyproheptadine. Only secretin has been investigated in several double-blind, placebo controlled studies, none of which showed benefit over placebo in any symptoms of autism (meta-analysis by Sturmey, 2005). Despite this lack of documented efficacy, many parents continue to believe that secretin is effective in treating the symptoms of autism. Few of the other treatments have been sufficiently studied, and those that have been have not substantiated effects on symptoms of autism. Side effects of these treatments include peripheral neuropathy (B6), cardiac arrhythmia (magnesium), renal stones (vitamin C), sedation and increased appetite (cyproheptadine).

Treatments directed at gastrointestinal dysfunction that is purported to be related to abnormal absorption of centrally active peptides from the diet that alter brain function include gluten and casein dietary restriction, digestive enzymes, and famotidine (Pepcid). Again, no double-blind, placebo controlled trials exist (although several are currently in progress), and randomized or open trials have shown mixed or negative results (Christison & Ivany, 2006). Side effects include deficiencies in calcium, vitamin D and protein intake, and gastrointestinal symptoms (Brudnak et al., 2002).

Treatments aimed at modulation of immune function include antibiotic, antifungal and/or antiviral medications, probiotics, intravenous human immune globulin, vitamin A supplementation, and withholding of vaccines. No double-blind, placebo controlled studies have been done on any of these treatments. Open studies of immune globulin have had mixed results and raise serious risks related to aseptic meningitis, renal failure, and infection. Additional risks associated with these treatments include the development of drug-resistant organisms in children treated with antibiotic, antifungal, and antiviral agents, as well as liver toxicity and bone marrow suppression. Vitamin A toxicity includes brain swelling and liver damage. As discussed in Chapter 2, no epidemiologic evidence exists that supports a causal association with vaccines and autism, although individual susceptibility to live vaccines such as MMR has been raised as a concern by Wakefield and colleagues (2002).

Removal of toxins such as heavy metals by chelation has become increasingly popular over the past several years, particularly as concern over the vaccine preservative thimerosal (ethyl mercury) and other environmental sources of mercury exposure have increased. No epidemiologic studies have shown an association between thimerosal and autism (Hansen & Ozonoff, 2003; Levy & Hyman, 2005), and currently only some flu vaccines continue to contain thimerosal in the United States. Chelation has generally been administered by intravenous or oral routes, although some children are being treated by skin cream or Epsom salt baths as chelators. A double-blind, placebo controlled study of lead chelation in nonautistic children did not find any differences in cognitive outcomes in children treated (Dietrich et al., 2004; O'Connor & Rich, 1999; Rogan et al., 2001), nor did a study in adults chelated for elevated mercury levels (England et al., 1994), although both groups treated had lowered levels of metals. No other controlled studies have been reported. Side effects include kidney and liver toxicity, depletion of essential minerals, and seizures.

Concluding Comments

School professionals in general and school psychologists in particular can play an important role in discussing alternative therapies when parents ask for information

or advice in making decisions. Promoting communication and collaboration between parents, medical providers, and school personnel is important in helping
parents make well-informed decisions about choosing treatments for their children. Supporting parents by reading and discussing information about alternative
treatments, discussing side effects, and participating in monitoring outcomes and
side effects if parents decide on alternative treatments are important ways that
school psychologists contribute to the care and safety of children. Encouraging
parents to take advantage of participating in well-designed studies of alternative
therapies is another important contribution of school psychologists who have the
trust of and frequent contact with families and children.

Appendix
Autism Resources

Valuable Information on the Internet

We encourage professionals to utilize resources available on the Internet. However, it is often difficult to discern which sites are most useful when a search yields hundreds of relevant sites. The following web sites are among those found to be most useful by the students, practitioners, and researchers whom we work with. The brief summaries indicate the emphasis of each site.

General Autism Information

Autism Society of America

http://www.autism-society.org

The Autism Society of America's web page provides an overview of the general characteristics and diagnosis of autism and subtypes of autism spectrum disorders. The page also briefly discusses possible causes of autism and explains outdated ones. Of particular interest is the description of typical individuals with autism. This description clearly addresses the variability and heterogeneity in autism symptomatology and dismisses common myths. The page briefly summarizes treatments of autism and provides useful resources and current news and events related to autism. This page is useful to get general information about etiology, epidemiology, assessment, and treatment of children with autism spectrum disorders.

Center for the Study of Autism

http://www.autism.org/overview.html

This site, presented by Stephen M. Edelson, Ph.D., of the Center for the Study of Autism in Salem, Oregon, provides a fairly thorough overview of autism. In addition to a description of major characteristics of autistic disorder, it also provides information regarding prevalence, subgroups and related disorders, etiology, sensory impairments, cognition, and interventions. This site discusses a variety of view points and theories and is written in a clear and concise manner. It provides basic information and is easy to read and understand.

Yale Developmental Disabilities Clinic

http://info.med.yale.edu/chldstdy/autism/index.html

The Yale Developmental Disabilities Clinic offers valuable information regarding the diagnosis and interventions of pervasive developmental disorders. The web site offers resources, publications, and links to web sites. A particularly valuable feature of the web site is the information regarding Frequently Asked Questions, which are listed in the PDD Information section. The responses are provided by knowledgeable and reputable experts.

University of Michigan Autism and Communication Disorders Center

http://www.umaccweb.com/

The Autism and Communication Disorders Center web site at the University of Michigan provides information regarding research, education, diagnostic tools, and on-line resources. The summaries of the *ADOS*, *ADI-R*, and *SCQ* diagnostic tools are valuable in understanding each of these assessments, including an annotated bibliography for each. The center also provides training opportunities for professionals.

Etiology

Genetics: Serotonin

http://www.pslgroup.com/dg/24fae.htm

This web site summarizes the 1997 findings of scientists at the University of Chicago Medical Center, Children's Hospital Research Center in San Diego, and the University of California at San Diego who have been investigating the genetic causes of autism. Drawing from previous research implicating abnormal serotonin levels in the development of autism, researchers have found a genetic marker involved in serotonin levels in people diagnosed with autism. The study integrates genetic and biochemical issues elucidating some of the complex issues behind the diverse symptoms of autism.

Neuroanatomy: Cerebral Abnormalities

http://www.autism.org/cerebel.html

The Center for the Study of Autism in Salem, Oregon, provides a summary of Dr. Eric Courchesne's work on cerebellar abnormalities in people with autism. The author describes cerebellar abnormalities identified through magnetic resonance imaging and speculates on the possible role of these abnormalities in producing autistic symptoms. It is particularly useful as he describes the possible mechanisms involved and the behavioral manifestations of cerebral dysfunction. The summary is brief and provides information on one of the many hypothesized causes of autism.

Limbic System

http://www.autism.org/limbic.html

This site presents information regarding the possible role of the limbic system in the development of autism. Reporting on research done by scientists at Harvard Medical School and Boston University School of Medicine, the author describes limbic system abnormalities that may account for the presence of autistic symptoms. He also provides insight into specific behavioral manifestations of limbic system deficit. He links damage to the amygdala and hippocampus to aggressive behavior and emotional expression as well as to stereotypic, self-stimulatory, and hyperactive behavior. The site is written clearly and concisely.

Neurochemistry and Brain Development

http://www.nimh.nih.gov/publicat/autism.cfm

This site provides a comprehensive discussion of autism. Detailed information about the development of the brain is presented, as well as a discussion about the many problems that can interfere with normal brain development. Research regarding abnormalities in the limbic system, abnormalities in neurotransmitters (e.g., serotonin), and differences in MRI brain activity are discussed. In addition, factors that affect brain development are mentioned, such as heredity and development during pregnancy. The site also discusses various approaches to treating individuals with autism. A variety of resources and agencies are listed. This site is very thorough and well written.

Autism Facts and Biomedical Research

http://www.nichd.nih.gov/autism/

A comprehensive overview of the general facts of autism and its biomedical etiologies is provided by the autism section in this official web site of the National

Institute of Child Health and Human Development (NICHD). The site provides convenient access to current news releases, which includes genetic, neurochemical, and neuroatomical research articles on autism. The controversial debate on secretin treatment is discussed in detail. The site also includes links to key NICHD publications on the general facts and multifaceted etiologies of autism. Additionally, the site discusses ongoing autism research projects at the national level. The site is well organized and informative, yet brief and concise. Parents, educators, and other professionals working with persons with autism will find this site a helpful resource for locating quick, at-a-glance fact sheets and research articles that address the current issues in autism.

Brain Abnormalities

http://www.conradsimon.org/WorkingPaper.shtml

This site is developed by the Conrad Simon Memorial Education Program, whose purpose is to promote interdisciplinary perspectives on Autism Spectrum Disorders (ASD). Each subtopic provides a review of the extant literature on the neurological link to autism. This site relates easy to read information on the neuroanatomical abnormalities to the specific symptoms of autism.

Purported Link with Vaccines

http://www.cdc.gov/nip/vacsafe/concerns/autism/autism-mmr.htm

This web site of the United States Centers for Disease Control and Prevention (CDC) provides valuable information regarding whether the measles-mumps-rubella (MMR) vaccine causes autism. The CDC emphasizes that current scientific evidence does not support the hypothesis that measles-mumps-rubella (MMR) vaccine, or any combination of vaccines, causes the development of autism. Independent groups of experts in the United States including the National Academy of Sciences Institute of Medicine, have carefully examined research addressing a possible link between MMR vaccine and autism. These reviews have concluded that the available epidemiologic evidence does not support a causal link between MMR vaccine and autism. The CDC web site includes links to the Institute of Medicine reports examining immunization safety.

Assessment

Developmental Disorders Clinic

http://psy-svr1.bsd.uchicago.edu/ddc/home.htm

This is the web site for the Developmental Disorders Clinic at the University of Chicago, which offers evaluation and treatment fee-based services to parents of children suspected of having and/or diagnosed with autism. This web site is useful in order to view current research in the areas of assessment, molecular genetics, and pharmacological treatments.

Overview of Assessment Procedures

http://www.behavior-consultant.com/aut-dx-devices.htm

This web site, provided by Clinical and Behavioral Consultants of Reinforcement Unlimited, lists and discusses an extensive number of assessment procedures taken from Best Practices for Designing and Delivering Effective Programs for Individuals with Autism Spectrum Disorders: Recommendations of the Collaborative Work Group on Autistic Spectrum Disorders, sponsored by the California Department of Education and Developmental Services (July 1997). Assessments such as the *Autism Diagnostic Interview-Revised* (ADI-R), *Pre-Linguistic Autism Diagnostic Observation Schedule* (PL-ADOS), *Childhood Autism Rating Scale* (CARS), *Autism Screening Instrument for Educational Planning* (2nd ed.) (ASIEP-2), and many others are described. Assessments in areas such as adaptive behavior, communication and cognitive skills, family stress and cohesiveness among others are provided. Information about the assessment's development, reported technical adequacy, and suggested use is also provided. This site is particularly useful for professionals seeking information on widely used assessments for autism.

Treatment

Koegel Autism Center at UC Santa Barbara

http://www.education.ucsb.edu/autism/

A description of the overall orientation of the Koegel Autism Center at the University of California, Santa Barbara is provided. The web page includes numerous resources for parents and practitioners interested in Pivotal Response Training. This paradigm maximizes the effectiveness of behavioral techniques by targeting the individual's strengths and pivotal behaviors, such as motivation, with the expectation that other behaviors will be positively impacted as well. Updated information on the Journal of Positive Behavioral Interventions is provided. Upcoming dates and locations of presentations by Drs. Robert and Lynn Kern Koegel and other center scholars are listed.

Treatment and Education of Autistic and Related Communication Handicapped Children

http://www.unc.edu/depts/teacch

Division TEACCH, a comprehensive program providing services to autistic individuals and their families presents a web site with various related topics. The site provides an overview of the program, detailed descriptions of their behaviorally-oriented treatment paradigm (TEACCH services), and concrete suggestions for parents and teachers for ways in which to provide optimum teaching environments for children with autism (Structured Teaching, Structuring for Success, Nonverbal Thinking, Communication, Imitation, and Play Skills from a Developmental Perspective). In addition, a review of current treatment approaches is presented (A Pediatric View of Treatment Options for Autistic Syndrome), as well as guidelines for evaluating treatment programs (Evaluation Guidelines When Considering Nontraditional Therapies in Autism).

Biomedical Research

http://www.autism-biomed.org/links.htm

This site belongs to the Autism Biomedical Information Network, which provides up-to-date and evidence-based information on the biomedical aspects of autism. In addition to links to on-line resources for professionals working with persons with autism, the site features an extensive list of commentaries on and links to research studies published from 1999 to the present. The site includes a wide range of topics, ranging from general information on the biomedical perspectives and treatment options of autism to the discourse on controversies such as vaccination and secretin treatment. The scientifically-oriented seeking the most recent news in the biomedical bases of autism will find this site informative, well-written, and user-friendly.

Association for Science in the Treatment of Autism

http://www.asatonline.org/

The Association for Science in the Treatment of Autism (ASAT) emphasizes science as the most objective, time-tested, and reliable approach in determining safe, effective autism treatments. ASAT supports all scientifically sound research on the prevention, treatment, and cure of autism, as well as all treatments for autism that are shown to be effective through solid scientific research, regardless of discipline or domain. This web site includes a library of electronic resources that may be downloaded, as well as on-line links to valuable organizations.

Autism and ABA Resources: The Childhood Learning Center

http://www.tclc.com/

This site contains resources offered by the Child Learning Center for home programs and professionals who are using applied behavior analysis (ABA) and discrete trial intervention methodology. A variety of resources can be obtained, including consultation for educators, parents, and other professionals who want to design behavioral strategies for children with autism. A particularly helpful component of this web site is a section entitled "15 Frequently Asked Questions about Autism and ABA." This section provides 15 great questions about autism and ABA, such as what is ABA, and how many hours of treatment are necessary.

Additional Resources for School Psychologists, Parents, and Other Professionals

Autism Resources

http://www.autism-resources.com

This web site presents a comprehensive list of resources for autism, including books, research papers, on-line discussions, organizations, and various other resources. Numerous links regarding pervasive developmental disabilities, including autism, are offered. This site provides parents, educators, and professionals seeking information about the epidemiology, etiology, and treatment of autism with a great place to start.

Information About PDD-NOS and Atypical PDD

http://www.patientcenters.com/autism/

This site belongs to the Autism Resource Center, which is a resource center for families of individuals with pervasive developmental disorders. In addition, information about basic neurology and diagnostic tools, such as the Autism Research Institute's Form E 2 Check List and the Childhood Autism Rating Scale, is discussed. This is a helpful site for information about individuals with PDD-NOS and Atypical PDD and for more specific information for parents and professionals regarding the autistic spectrum.

National Alliance for Autism Research

http://www.naar.org

The National Alliance for Autism Research (NAAR) is a nonprofit organization that is committed to researching the causes, prevention, effective treatments, and, ultimately, a cure for autism. The web site provides detailed information about biomedical research in autistic disorder. In addition, the site provides an on-line store with books about autism and educational materials for families and professionals. This is a well-organized web site. The online store is especially helpful for parents and educators who are attempting to gather materials about autism.

Professional Development in Autism

http://depts.washington.edu/pdacent/

With funding from the U.S. Department of Education, the Professional Development in Autism Center (PDA) offers training and support for school districts, families, and communities to ensure that students with ASD have access to high quality, evidence-based educational services in his or her local school district. This web site provides information regarding resources, workshops, and on-line courses for professionals seeking further training about working with children with autism.

M.I.N.D. Institute at University of California, Davis

http://www.ucdmc.ucdavis.edu/mindinstitute/

The M.I.N.D. Institute at the University of California, Davis, is an international, multidisciplinary research organization committed to collaboration to understand the causes and develop better treatments and ultimately cures for neurodevelopmental disorders. It is hoped that advances in neuroscience, molecular biology, genetics, pharmacology, and behavioral sciences enhance understanding of brain functions related to autism. This web site offers information regarding research and resources examining autism and other neurodevelopmental disorders.

References

Akshoomoff, N., Lord, C., Lincoln, A.J., Courchesne, R.Y., Carper, R.A., Townsend, J., & Courchesne, E. (2004). Outcome classification of preschool children with autism spectrum disorders using MRI brain measures. *Journal of the American Academy of Child and Adolescent Psychiatry, 43*, 349–357.

Akshoomoff, N., Pierce, K., & Courchesne, E. (2002). The neurobiological basis of autism from a developmental perspective. *Development and Psychopathology, 14*, 613–634.

Aman, M.G., & Langworthy, K.S. (2000). Pharmacotherapy for hyperactivity in children with autism and other pervasive developmental disorders. *Journal of Autism and Developmental Disorders, 30*, 451–459.

American Academy of Pediatrics. (2001a). The pediatrician's role in the diagnosis and management of autistic spectrum disorder in children. *Pediatrics, 107*, 1221–1226.

American Academy of Pediatrics. (2001b). Counseling families who choose complementary and alternative medicine for their childe with chronic illness and disability. *Pediatrics, 107*, 598–601.

American Psychiatric Association (1980). *Diagnostic and statistical manual of mental disorders* (3rd ed.). Washington, DC: American Psychiatric Association.

American Psychiatric Association (1987). *Diagnostic and statistical manual of mental disorders* (3rd ed., rev.). Washington, DC: American Psychiatric Association.

American Psychiatric Association (2000). *Diagnostic and statistical manual of mental disorders* (4th ed., text rev.). Washington, DC: American Psychiatric Association.

Asperger, H. (1944). "Autistichan Psychopathen" im kindersalter. ["Autistic psychopathy" in childhood.]. *Archive fur Psychiatrie und Nervenkrankheiten, 117*, 76–136.

Attwood, T. (1998). *Asperger's syndrome: A guide for parents and professionals.* London: Kingsley.

Baird, G., Cass, H., & Slonims, V. (2003). Diagnosis of autism. *BMJ, 327*, 488–493.

Baird, G., Charman, T., Baron-Cohen, S., Cox, A., Swettenham, J., Wheelwright, S., & Drew, A. (2000). A screening instrument for autism at 18 months of age: A 6-year follow-up study. *Journal of the American Academy of Child and Adolescent Psychiatry, 39*, 694–702.

Barbaresi, W.J., Katusic, S.K., Colligan, R.C., Weaver, A.L., & Jacobsen, S.J. (2005). In incidence of autism in Olmsted County, Minnesota, 1976–1997: Results from a population-based study. *Archives of Pediatrics & Adolescent Medicine, 159*, 37–44.

Baron-Cohen, S., Allen, J., & Gillberg, C. (1992). Can autism be detected at 18 months? The needle, the haystack, and the CHAT. *British Journal of Psychiatry, 161*, 839–843.

Baron-Cohen, S., Cox, A., Baird, G., Swettenham. J., Nightingale, N., Morgan, K., Drew, A., & Charman, T. (1996). Psychological markers in the detection of autism in infancy in a large population. *British Journal of Psychiatry, 168*, 158–163.

Baron-Cohen, S., Wheelwright, S., Cox, A., Baird, G., Charman, T., Swettenham, J., Drew, A., Coehring, P. (2000). Early identification of autism by the CHecklist for Autism in Toddlers (CHAT). *Journal of the Royal Society of Medicine, 93*, 521–525.

Barton, M. & Volkmar, F. (1998). How commonly are known medical conditions associated with autism? *Journal of Autism and Developmental Disorders, 28*, 273–278.

Bauminger, N. (2002). The facilitation of social-emotional understanding and social interaction in high-functioning children with autism: Intervention outcomes. *Journal of Autism and Developmental Disorders, 32*, 283–298.

Bayley, N. (1993). *The Bayley Scales of Infant Development* (2nd ed.). San Antonio, TX, Psychological Corporation.

Berument, S.K., Rutter, M., Lord, C., Pickles, A., & Bailey, A. (1999). Autism screening questionnaire: Diagnostic validity. *British Journal of Psychiatry, 175*, 444–451.

Blair, K.A. (2003). Test review of the Asperger Syndrome Diagnostic Scale. From B.S. Plake, J.C. Impara, & R.A. Spies (Eds.), *The Fifteenth Mental Measurements Yearbook* [Electronic version]. Retrieved December 23, 2003, from the Buros Institute's *Test Reviews Online* web site: http://www.unl.edu/buros

Bölte, S., & Poustka, F. (2002). The relation between general cognitive level and adaptive behavior domains in individuals with autism with and without co-morbid mental retardation. *Child Psychiatry and Human Development, 33*, 165–172.

Bondy, A.S., & Frost, L.A. (1994). The picture Exchange Communication System. *Focus on Autistic Behavior, 9*, 1–19.

Bondy, A. and Frost, L. (2002) *A picture's worth: PECS and other visual communication strategies in autism*. Maryland: Woodbine House.

Bostic, J., & King, B. (2005). Autism spectrum disorders: Emerging pharmacotherapy. *Expert Opinion on Emerging Drugs, 10*, 521–536.

Bray, M.A., Kehle, T.J., & Theodore, L.A. (2002). Case study of childhood disintegrative disorder—Heller's syndrome. *Psychology in the Schools, 39*, 101–109.

Brereton, A.V., Tonge, B.J., MacKinnon, A.J., Einfeld, S.L. (2002). Screening young people for autism with the Developmental Behavior Checklist. *Journal of the American Academy of Child and Adolescent Psychiatry, 41*, 1369–1375.

Bricker, D., & Squires, J. (1994). *Ages and Stages Questionnaire*. Baltimore, MD: Paul H. Brooks.

Brigance, A. (1986). *The BRIGANCE® Screens*. North Billerica, MA: Curriculum Associates.

Brock, S.E. (1999). The diagnosis of attention-deficit/hyperactivity disorder in childhood. *The California School Psychologist, 4*, 18–29.

Brock, S.E. (2004, Summer). Testing accommodations for the student with an ASD. *CASP Today: Quarterly Newsletter of the California Association of School Psychologists, 53* (3), 1, 4, 12.

Brown, L., Sherbenou, R.J., & Johnson, S.K. (1997). *Test of Nonverbal Intelligence-3* (TONI-*3*): *A Language-Free Measure of Intelligence, Aptitude and Reasoning*. Austin, TX, PRO-ED.

Brownell, R. (2000). *Expressive One-Word Picture Vocabulary Test*. Novato, CA: Academic Therapy Publications.

Brudnak, M.A., Rimland, B., Kerry, R.E., Dailey, M., Taylor, R., Stayton, B., Waickman, F., Waickman, M., Pangborn, J., & Buchholz, I. (2002). Enzyme-based therapy for autism spectrum disorders-is it worth another look? *Medical Hypothesis, 58,* 422–428.

Bryson, S.E., Rogers, S.J., & Fombonne, E. (2003). Autism spectrum disorders: Early detection, intervention, education, and psychopharmacological management. *Canadian Journal of Psychiatry, 48,* 506–516.

Burgemeister, B.B., Blum, L.H., & Lorge, I. (1972*). Columbia Mental Maturity Scale* (3rd ed.). New York: Harcourt Brace.

Buxhoeveden, D.P., & Casanova, M.F. (2002). The minicolumn hypothesis in neuroscience. *Brain, 125,* 935–951.

California Department of Developmental Services (2002). *Autistic Spectrum Disorders: Best Practice Guidelines for Screening, Diagnosis and Assessment.* Sacramento, CA. Retrieved August 11, 2003 from http://www.ddhealthinfo.org

Carr, E.G., Levin, L., McConnachie, G., Carlson, J.I., Kemp, D.C., & Smith, C.E. (1994). *Communication-Based Intervention for Problem Behavior: A User's Guide for Producing Positive Change.* Baltimore MD: Brookes.

Carter, A.S., Vokmar, F.R., Sparrow, S.S., Wang, J., Lord, C., Dawson, G., Fombonne, E., Loveland, K., Mesibov, G., & Schopler, E. (1998). The Vineland adaptive behavior scales: Supplemental norms for individuals with autism. *Journal of Autism and Developmental Disorders, 28,* 287–302.

Casanova, M.F., Buxhoeveden, D.P., Switala, A.E., & Roy, E. (2002). Minicolumnar pathology in autism. *Neurology, 58,* 428–432.

Centers for Disease Control and Prevention. (1998). Prevalence of autism in Brick Township, New Jersey. Atlanta, GA. Retrieved November 30, 2004, from http://www.cdc.gov/ncbddd/pub/BrickReport.pdf

Chakrabarti, S., & Fombonne, E. (2001). Pervasive developmental disorders in preschool children. *JAMA, 285,* 3093–3099.

Christison, G.W., & Ivany, K. (2006). Elimination diets in autistic spectrum disorders: Any wheat amidst the chaff? *Journal of Developmental Behavioral Pediatrics* (in press).

Ciaranello, A.L., & Ciaranello, R.D. (1995). The neurobiology of infantile autism. *Annual Review of Neurosciences, 18,* 101–128.

Courchesne, E., Carper, R., & Akshoomoff, N. (2003). Evidence of brain overgrowth in the first year of life in autism. *JAMA, 290,* 337–334.

Croen, L.A., Grether, J.K., & Selvin, S. (2002). The changing prevalence of autism in California. *Journal of Autism and Developmental Disorders, 32,* 207–215.

Cummings, C. (2004). *School psychologists' knowledge of autism.* Unpublished Masters Thesis, California State University Sacramento.

De Giacomo, A., & Fombonne, E. (1998). Parental recognition of developmental abnormalities in autism. *European Child & Adolescent Psychiatry, 7,* 131–136.

Deisinger, J.A. (2001). Diagnosis and assessment of autistic spectrum disorders. In T. Wahlberg, F. Obiakor, S. Burkhardt, & A.F. Rotatori (Eds.), *Autistic spectrum disorders: Educational and clinical interventions* (Advances in Special Education, Vol. 14, pp. 181–209). New York: JAI (Elsevier Science).

Dietrich, K.N., Ware, J.H., Salganik, M., Radcliffe, J., Rogan, W.J., Rhoads, G.G., Fay, M.E., Davoli, C.T., Denckla, M.B., Bornschein, R.L., Schwarz, D., Dockery, D.W., Adubato, S., & Jones, R.L. (2004). Effect of chelation therapy on the neuropsychological and behavioral development of lead-exposed children after school entry. *Pediatrics, 114,* 19–26.

Dunn, L.M., & Dunn, L.M. (1997). *The Peabody Picture Vocabulary Test* (3rd ed.). Circle Pines, MN: American Guidance Service.

Edelson, M.G. (1995). *Autism-Related Disorders in DSM-IV.* Center for the Study of Autism. Retrieved December 31, 2004, from www.autism.org/dsm.html

Ehlers, S., & Gillberg, G. (1993). The epidemiology of Asperger syndrome: A total population study. *Journal of Child Psychology and Psychiatry, 34*, 1327–1350.

Ehlers, S., Gillberg, G., & Wing, L. (1999). A screening questionnaire for Asperger syndrome and other high functioning autism spectrum disorders in school age children. *Journal of Autism and Developmental Disorders, 29*, 129–141.

Ehlers, S., Nydén, A., Gillberg, C., Dahlgren Sandberg, A., Dahlgre, S., Hjelmquist, E., & Odén, A. (1997). Asperger syndrome, autism and attention disorders: A comparative study of the cognitive profiles of 120 children. *Journal of Child Psychiatry and Psychology, 38*, 207–217.

Einfeld, S.L., & Tonge, B.J. (1995). The Developmental Behaviour Checklist: The development and validation of an instrument to assess behavioural and emotional disturbance in children and adolescents with mental retardation. *Journal of Autism and Developmental Disorders, 25*, 81–104.

Elliott, C. (1990). *Differential Abilities Scale.* San Antonio, TX: Psychological Corporation.

Englund, G. S., Dahlqvist, R., Lindelof, B., Soderman, E., Jonzon, B., Vesterberg, O., & Larsson, K. S. (1994). DMSA administration to patients with allege mercury poisoning from dental amalgams: A placebo-controlled study. *Journal of Dental Research, 73*, 620–628.

Exploring autism. (2002). *A look at the genetics of autism.* Retrieved December 7, 2004 from http://www.exploringautism.org/genetics/

Filipek, P.A., Accardo, P.J., Baranek, G.T., Cook E.H., Dawson, G., Gordon, B., Gravel, J.S., Johnson, C.P., Kallen, R.J., Levy, S.E., Minshew, N.J., Prizant, B.M., Rapin, I., Rogers, S.J., Stone, W.L., Teplin, S., Tuchman, R.F., & Volkmar, F.R. (1999). The screening and diagnosis of autistic spectrum disorders. *Journal of Autism and Developmental Disorders, 29*, 439–484.

Filipek, P.A., Accardo, P.J., Asshwal, S., Baranek, G.T., Cook, E.H., Dawson, G., Gordon, B., Gravel, J.S., Johnson, C.P., Kallen, R.J., Levy, S.E., Minshew, N.J., Ozonoff, S., Prizant, B.M., Rapin, I., Rogers, S.I., Stone, W.I., Teplin, S.W., Tuchman, R.F., & Volkmar, F.R. (2000). Practice parameter: Screening and diagnosis of autism. *Neurology, 55*, 468–479.

Fogt, J.B., Miller, D.N., & Zirkel, P.A. (2003). Defining autism: Professional best practice and published case law. *Journal of School Psychology, 41*, 201–216.

Fombonne, E. (1999). The epidemiology of autism: A review. *Psychological Medicine, 29*, 769–786.

Fombonne, E. (2003a). Epidemiology of pervasive developmental disorders. *Trends in Evidence-Based Neuropsychiatry, 5*, 29–36.

Fombonne, E. (2003b). The prevalence of autism. *JAMA, 289*, 87–89.

Fombonne, E. (2003c, September). Modern views of autism. *The Canadian Journal of Psychiatry, 48*, 503–505.

Fombonne, E., & Tidmarsh, L. (2003). Epidemiologic data on Asperger disorder. *Child and Adolescent Psychiatric Clinics of North America, 12*, 15–21.

Freeman, B.J., Del'Homme, M., Guthrie, D., & Zhang, F. (1999). Vineland adaptive behavior scale scores as a function of age and initial IQ in 210 autistic children. *Journal of Autism and Developmental Disorders, 29*, 379–384.

Frith, U. (1989). *Autism: Explaining the Enigma.* Cambridge, MA: Blackwell.

Garcia Winner, M. (2000). *Inside Out: What Makes a Person with Social Cognitive Deficits Tick?* San Jose, CA: Winner.

Garcia Winner, M. (2006). *Think social! A social thinking curriculum for school-age students*. Retrieved January 20, 2006, from www.socialthinking.com

Garretson, H.B., Fein, D., & Waterhouse, L. (1990). Sustained attention in children with autism. *Journal of Autism and Developmental Disorders, 20*, 101–114.

Gernsbacher, M.A., Dawson, M., & Goldsmith, H.H. (2005). Three reasons not to believe in an autism epidemic. *Current Directions in Psychological Science, 14*, 55–58.

Ghaziuddin, M. (2000). Autism in mental retardation. *Current Opinion in Psychiatry, 13*, 481–484.

Ghaziuddin, M., & Mountain-Kimchi, K. (2004). Defining the intellectual profile of Asperger syndrome: Comparison with high-functioning autism. *Journal of Autism and Developmental Disorders, 34*, 279–284.

Gillberg, C., & Wing, L. (1999). Autism: Not an extremely rare disorder. *Acta Psychiatrica Scandinavica, 99*, 399–406.

Gilliam, J.E. (1995). *Gilliam Autism Rating Scale (GARS)*. Austin, TX: Pro-Ed.

Gilliam, J.E. (2005). *Gilliam Autism Rating Scale: Second Edition* (GARS-2). Austin, TX: Pro-Ed.

Glascoe, F.P. (1997). *Parents' Evaluation of Developmental Status (PEDS)*. Nashville, TN: Ellsworth & Vandermeer Press.

Glasson, E.J., Bower, C., Peterson, B., de Klerk, N., Chancey, G., & Hallmayer, J.F. (2004). Perinatal factors in the development of autism: A population study. *Archives of General Psychiatry, 61*, 618–627.

Goin, R.P., & Myers, B.J. (2004). Characteristics of infantile autism: Moving toward earlier detection. *Focus on Autism and Other Developmental Disabilities, 19*, 5–12.

Goldstein H., & Strain, P.S. (1988). Peers as communication intervention agents: Some new strategies and research findings. *Topics in Language Disorders, 9*, 44–57.

Goldstein, H., Kaczmarek, L., Pennington, R., & Shafer, K. (1992). Peer-mediated intervention: Attending to, commenting on, and acknowledging the behavior of preschoolers with autism. *Journal of Applied Behavior Analysis, 25*, 289–305.

Goodwin-Jones, B.J., & Solomon, M. (2003). Contributions of psychology. In S. Ozonoff, S.J. Rogers, & R.L. Hendren (Eds.), *Autism spectrum disorders: A research review for practitioners* (pp. 55–85). Washington, DC: American Psychiatric Press.

Greenspan, S.I. (2000). *Building healthy minds: The six experiences that create intelligence and emotional growth in babies and young children*. New York: Da Capo.

Greenspan, S.I., & Weider, S. (1997). Developmental patterns and outcomes in infants and children with disorders in relating and communicating: A chart review of 200 cases of children with autistic spectrum diagnoses. *Journal of Developmental and Learning Disorders, 1*, 87–141.

Gutstein, S.G., & Sheely, R.K. (2002). *Relationship Development Intervention with Young Children: Social and Emotional Development Activities for Asperger Syndrome, Autism, PDD, and NLD*. London: Jessica Kingsley.

Hagerman, R.J. (2002). Medical follow up and pharmacotherapy. In R.J. Hagerman & P.J. Hagerman (Eds.), *Fragile X Syndrome: Diagnosis, Treatment and Research* (3rd ed., pp. 287–338). Baltimore, MD: Johns Hopkins University Press.

Hagerman, R.J., Riddle, J.E., Roberts, L.S., Breese, K. & Fulton, M. (1995). A survey of the efficacy of clonidine in Fragile X syndrome. *Developmental Brain Dysfunction, 8*, 336–344.

Handen, B.L., Johnson, C.R., & Lubetsky, M. (2000). Efficacy of methylphenidate among children with autism and symptoms of attention-deficit hyperactivity disorder. *Journal of Autism and Developmental Disorders, 30*, 245–255.

Handleman, J.S., & Harris, S.L. (Eds). (2001). *Preschool Education Programs for Children with Autism* (2nd ed.). Austin, TX: Pro-Ed.

Hansen, R.L., & Hagerman, R.J. (2003). Contributions of pediatrics. In S. Ozonoff, S.J. Rogers, & R.L. Hendren (Eds.), *Autism Spectrum Disorders: A Research Review for Practitioners* (pp. 87–109). Washington, DC: American Psychiatric Press.

Harris, S.L., Handleman, J.S., Arnold, M.S., & Gordon, R.F. (2001). The Douglass developmental disabilities center: Two models of service delivery. In J.S. Handleman & S.L. Harris (Eds.), *Preschool Education Programs for Children with Autism* (2nd ed., pp. 233–260). Austin, TX: Pro-Ed.

Harrington, J., Rosen, L., Garnecho, A., & Patrick, P.A. (2006). Parental perception and use of CAM practices for children with autistic spectrum disorder in private practice. *Journal of Developmental Behavioral Pediatrics* (in press).

Harrower, J., & Dunlap, G. (2001). Including children with autism in general education classrooms: A review of effective strategies. *Behavior Modification, 25* (5), 762–784.

Hendren, R.L. (2003). Contributions of the psychiatrist. In S. Ozonoff, S.J. Rogers, & R.L. Hendren (Eds.), *Autism Spectrum Disorders: A Research Review for Practitioners* (pp. 37–53). Washington, DC: American Psychiatric Press.

Hill, A., Bölte, S., Petrova, G., Beltcheva, D., Tacheva, S., & Poustka, R. (2001). Stability and interpersonal agreement of the interview-based diagnosis of autism. *Psychopathology, 34,* 187–191.

Howlin, P., & Asgharian, A. (1999). The diagnosis of autism and Asperger syndrome: Findings from a survey of 770 families. *Developmental Medicine and Child Neurology, 41,* 834–839.

Howlin, P., Goode, S., Hutton, J., & Rutter, M. (2004). Adult outcomes for children with autism. *Journal of Child Psychology and Psychiatry, 45,* 212–229.

Hussman, J.P. (2001). Suppressed GABAergic inhibition as a common factor in suspected etiologies of autism. *Journal of Autism and Developmental Disorders, 31,* 247–248.

Immunization Safety Review Committee. (2004). *Immunization Safety Review: Vaccines and Autism.* Washington, DC: The National Academy Press. Retrieved August 20, 2005, from http://www.nap.edu/catalog/10997.html

Ireton, H. (1992). *Child Development Inventories.* Minneapolis, MN: Behavior Science Systems.

Jellinek, M., Patel, B.P., & Froehle, M.C. (Eds.). (2002). Pervasive developmental disorders. In *Bright Futures in Practice: Mental Health* (Vol. I., Practice guide, pp. 317–330). Arlington, VA: National Center for Education in Maternal and Child Health.

Joshi, I., Percy, M., & Brown, I. (2004). Advances in understanding causes of autism and effective interventions. *Journal on Developmental Disabilities, 9*(2), 1–27.

Kabot, S., Masi, W., & Segal, M. (2003). Advances in the diagnosis and treatment of autism spectrum disorders. *Professional Psychology: Research and Practice, 34,* 26–33.

Kanner, L. (1943). Autistic disturbances of affective contact. *Nervous Child, 2,* 217–250.

Kaufman, A.S., & Kaufman, N.L. (2004). *Kaufman Assessment Battery for Children, Second Edition.* Circle Pines, MN: American Guidance Services.

Kielinen, M., Rantala, H., Timonen, E., Linna, S.L., & Moilanen, I. (2000). Associated medical disorders and disabilities in children with autistic disorder: A population based study. *Autism, 8,* 49–60.

Kielinen, M., Linna, S.L., & Moilanen, I. (2000). Autism in northern Finland. *European Child and Adolescent Psychiatry, 9,* 162–167.

Klin, A., Carter, A.S., & Sparrow, S.S. (1997). Psychological assessment of children with autism. In D.J. Cohen & F.R. Volkmar (Eds.), *Handbook of Autism and Pervasive Developmental Disorders* (2nd ed., pp. 418–427). New York: Wiley.

Klinger, L.G., & Renner, P. (2000). Performance-based measures in autism: Implications for diagnosis, early detection, and identification of cognitive profiles. *Journal of Clinical Child Psychology, 29,* 479–493.

Klotz, M.B., & Nealis, L. (2005, February). The new IDEA: A summary of significant reforms. *Communiqué: Newspaper of the National Association of School Psychologists, 33*(4), 1, 4–5.

Koegel, R.L., & Koegel, L.K. (1995). *Teaching Children with Autism: Strategies for Initiating Positive Interactions and Improving learning Opportunities.* Baltimore, MD: Paul H. Brooks Publishing Company.

Koegel, R.L., & Koegel, L.K. (2006). *Pivotal Response Treatments for Autism: Communication, Social and Academic Development.* Baltimore MD: Paul H. Brookes Publishing Company, Inc.

Koegel, L.K., Koegel, R.L., Frea, W.D. & Fredeen, R.M. (2001). Identifying early intervention targets for children with autism in inclusive school settings. *Behavior Modification, 25* (5), 745–761.

Koegel, L.K., Koegel, R.L., & Smith, A. (1997). Variables related to differences in standardized test outcomes for children with autism. *Journal of Autism and Developmental Disorders, 27,* 233–243.

Koegel, L.K., Koegel, R.L., &. Carter, C.M. (1998). Pivotal responses and the natural language teaching paradigm. *Seminars in Speech and Language, 19,* 355–371.

Koegel, L.K., Koegel, R.L., Harrower, J.K., & Carter, C. (1999). Pivotal response intervention: overview of approach. *Journal of the Association of Persons with Severe Handicaps, 24,* 174–185.

Kohrt, B. (2004, Winter). School psychologists respond to ASD survey. *CASP Today, 53*(1), 4.

Kovacs, M. (1982). *The Children's Depression Inventory.* North Tonawanda, NY: Multi-Health Systems.

Krasny, L., Williams, B.J., Provencal, S., & Ozonoff, S. (2003). Social skills interventions for the autism spectrum: Essential ingredients and a model curriculum. *Child and Adolescent Psychiatric Clinics of North America, 12,* 107–122.

Levy, S.E., & Hyman, S.L. (2005). Novel treatments for autistic spectrum disorders. *MRDD Research Reviews, 11,* 131–142.

Levy, S.E., Mandell, D.S., Merhar, S., Ittenbach, R.F., & Pinto-Martin, J.A. (2003). Use of complementary and alternative medicine among children recently diagnosed with autistic spectrum disorder. *Journal of Developmental and Behavioral Pediatrics, 24,* 418–423.

Lincoln, A.J., Allen, M.H., & Kilman, A. (1995). The assessment and interpretation of intellectual abilities in people with autism. In E. Schopler & G.B. Mesibov (Eds.), *Learning and Cognition in Autism* (pp. 89–117). New York: Plenum.

Loftin, R., & Lantz, J. (2003). Cognitive assessment of children with autism spectrum disorders. *The School Psychologist, 57*(3), 105–108.

London E., & Etzel, R.A. (2000). The environment as an etiologic factor in autism: New directions for research. *Environmental Health Perspectives Supplements, 108*(S3).

Retrieved December 4, 2004, from http://ehp.niehs.nih.gov/members/2000/suppl-3/401-404london/london-full.html

Lord, C., Risi, S., Lambrecht, L., Cook, E.H., Jr., Leventhal. B.L., DiLavore, P.C., Pickles, A., & Rutter, M. (2000). The autism diagnostic observation schedule-generic: A standard measure of social and communication deficits associated with the spectrum of autism. *Journal of Autism and Developmental Disorders, 30*, 205–223.

Lord, C., Rutter, M., DiLavore, P.C., & Risi, S. (1999a). *Autism Diagnostic Observation Schedule-WPS (WPS Edition)*, Los Angeles, CA: Western Psychological Services.

Lord, C., Rutter, M., DiLavore, P.C., & Risi, S. (1999b). The autism diagnostic observation schedule-generic: A standard measure of social and communication deficits associated with the spectrum of autism. *Journal of Autism and Developmental Disorders, 30*, 205–223.

Lotter, V. (1967). Epidemiology of autistic conditions in young children, II: Some characteristics of parents and their children. *Social Psychiatry, 1*, 163–173.

Lovaas, O.I. (1987). Behavioral treatment and normal educational and intellectual functioning in young autistic children. *Journal of Consulting and Clinical Psychology, 55*, 3–9.

Madsen, K.M., Hviid, A., Vestergaard, M., Schendel, D., Whofahrt, J., Thorsen, P., Olsen, J., & Melbye, M. (2002). A population-based study of measles, mumps, and rubella vaccination and autism. *The New England Journal of Medicine, 347*, 1477–1482.

Magnusson, P., & Saemundsen, E. (2001). Prevalence of autism in Iceland. *Journal of Autism and Developmental Disorders, 31*, 153–163.

Malhotra, S., & Gupta, N. (2002). Childhood disintegrative disorder: Re-examination of the current concept. *European Child and Adolescent Psychiatry, 11*, 108–114.

Marcus, L.M., Flagler, S., & Robinson, S. (2001). Assessment of children with autism. In R.J. Simeonsson & S.L. Rosenthal (Eds.), *Psychological and Developmental Assessment: Children with Disabilities and Chronic Conditions* (pp. 267–291). New York: Guilford Press.

Marcus, L.M., Lansing, M., & Schopler, E. (1993). Assessment of children with autism and pervasive developmental disorder. In J.L. Culbertson & D.J. Willis (Eds.), *Testing Young Children: A Reference Guide of Developmental, Psychoeducational, and Psychosocial Assessments* (pp. 319–344). Austin, TX: Pro-Ed.

Marcus, L., Schopler, E., & Lord, C. (2001). TEACCH services for preschool children. In J.S. Handleman & L.S. Harris (Eds.), *Preschool Education Programs for Children with Autism* (2nd ed., pp. 215–232). Austin, TX: Pro-Ed.

Mastergeorge, A.M., Rogers, S.J., Corbett, B.A., & Solomon, M. (2003). Nonmedical interventions for autism spectrum disorders. In S. Ozonoff, S.J. Rogers, & R.L. Hendren (Eds.), *Autism Spectrum Disorders: A Research Review for Practitioners* (pp. 133–160). Washington, DC: American Psychiatric Press.

Matsuishi, T., Yamashita, Y., Ohtani, Y., Ornitz, E., Kuriya, N., Murakami, Y., Fukuda, S., Hashimoto, T., & Yamashita, F. (1999). Incidence of and risk factors for autistic disorder in neonatal intensive care unit survivors. *Journal of Autism and Developmental Disorders, 29*, 161–166.

Mayes, S.D., & Calhoun, S.L. (2003). Ability profiles in children with autism. *Autism, 7*, 65–80.

McClannahan, L.E., & Krantz, P.J. (2001). Behavior analysis and intervention for preschoolers at the Princeton Child Development Institute. In J.S. Handleman & L.S. Harris (Eds.), *Preschool Education Programs for Children with Autism* (2nd ed., pp. 191–214). Austin, TX: Pro-Ed.

ambler, D., Rogers, S.J., & Wehner, E.A. (2001). Can the checklist for autism in toddlers differentiate young children with autism from those with developmental delays? *Journal of the American Academy of Child & Adolescent Psychiatry, 40*, 1457–1463.

Schopler, E., Mesibov, G.B., & Hearsey, K. (1995). Structured teaching in the TEACCH system. In E. Schopler & G.B. Mesibov (Eds.), *Learning and Cognition in Autism* (pp. 243–268). New York: Plenum.

Schopler, E., Lansing, M.D., Reichler, R.J., & Marcus, L.M. (2005). *Psychoeducational Profile: Third Edition (PEP-3)*. Austin, TX: Pro Ed.

Schopler, E., Reichler, R., & Lansing, M. (1980). *Individualized Assessment and Treatment for Autistic and Developmentally Disabled Children: Vol. 2, Teaching Strategies for Parents and Professionals*. Austin, TX: Pro Ed.

Schopler, E., Reichler, R., & Renner, B. (1988). *The Childhood Autism Rating Scale (CARS)*. Los Angles, CA: Western Psychological Services.

Schreibman, L. (2000). Intensive behavioral/psychoeducational treatments for autism: research needs and future directions. *Journal of Autism and Developmental Disorders, 30*, 373–378.

Schreibman, L. (2005). *The Science and Fiction of Autism*. Cambridge, MA: Harvard University Press.

Schreibman, L., & Ingersoll, B. (2005). Behavioral interventions to promote learning in individuals with autism. F. Volkmar, R. Paul, A. Klin, and D. Cohen (Eds.). *Handbook of Autism and Pervasive Developmental Disorders* (3rd ed., pp. 882–896). Hoboken, NJ: Wiley.

Schreibman, L., & Koegel, R.L. (2005). Training for parents of children with autism: Pivotal responses, generalization, and individualization of interventions. In E.D. Hibbs & P.S. Jensen (Eds.), *Psychosocial Treatment for Child and Adolescent Disorders: Empirically Based Strategies for Clinical Practice* (2nd ed., pp. 605–631). Washington, DC: American Psychological Association.

Scott, F.J., Baron-Cohen, S., Bolton, P., & Brayne, C. (2002). The CAST (Childhood Asperger Syndrome Test): Preliminary development of a UK screen for mainstream primary-school-age children, *Autism, 6*, 9–31.

Shriver, M.D., Allen, K.D., & Mathews, J.R. (1999). Effective assessment of the shared and unique characteristics of children with autism. *School Psychology Review, 28*, 538–558.

Siegel, B. (1996). *The World of the Autistic Child: Understanding and Treating Autistic Spectrum Disorders*. New York: Oxford University Press.

Siegel, B. (2004). *Pervasive Developmental Disorder Screening Test II: Early Childhood Screener for Autistic Spectrum Disorders*. San Antonio, TX: PsychCorp.

Siegel, D.J., Minshew, N.J., & Goldstein, G. (1996). Wechsler IQ profiles in diagnosis of high-functioning autism. *Journal of Autism and Developmental Disorders, 26*, 389–406.

Smith, T., Eikeseth, S., Klevstrand, M., & Lovaas, O.I. (1997). Intensive behavioral treatment for preschoolers with severe mental retardation and pervasive developmental disorder. *American Journal of Mental Retardation, 102*, 238–249.

Smith, T., Groen, A.D., & Wynn, J.W. (2000). Randomized trial of intensive early intervention for children with pervasive developmental disorder. *American Journal of Mental Retardation, 105*, 269–285.

South, M., William, B.J., McMahon, W.M., Owley, T., Filipek, P.A., Shernoff, E., Corsello, C., Lainhart, J.E., Landa, R., & Ozonoff, S. (2002). Utility of the Gilliam Autism Rating Scale in research and clinical populations. *Journal of Autism and Developmental Disorders, 32*, 593–599.

McDougle, C.J., Naylor, S.T., Cohen, D.J., Aghajanian, G.K., Heninger, G.R., & Price, L.H. (1996a). Effects of tryptophan depletion in drug-free adults with autistic disorder. *Archives of General Psychiatry, 53*, 993–1000.

McDougle, C.J., Naylor, S.T., Cohen, D.J., Volkmar, F.R., Heninger, G.R., & Price, L.H. (1996b). A double-blind, placebo-controlled study of fluvoxamine in adults with autistic disorder. *Archives of General Psychiatry, 53*, 1001–1008.

McEachin, J.J., Smith, T., & Lovaas, O.I. (1993). Long-term outcome for children with autism who received early intensive behavioral treatment. *American Journal of Mental Retardation, 97*, 359–372.

McGee, G., Morrier, M., & Daly, T. (1999). An incidental teaching approach to early intervention for toddlers with autism. *Journal of the Association for Persons with Severe Handicaps, 24*, 133–146.

McKinney, M. (2002, February 11). Brain abnormalities identified in autistic brains. *Reuters Health*. Retrieved December 28, 2004, from http://www.hbot4u.com/autism4.html

Mesibov, G.B. (1986). A cognitive program for teaching social behaviors to verbal autistic adolescents and adults. In E. Shopler, G.B. Mesibov, & J.T. Kunce, *Social Behavior in Autism* (pp. 265–283). New York: Plenum.

Mesibov, G.B., Schopler, E., Schaffer, B., & Landrus, R. (1988). *Adolescent and adult psychoeducational profile (AAPEP)*. Austin, TX: Pro Ed.

Mesibov, G.B., Shea, V., & Schopler, E., (2005). *The TEACCH approach to autism spectrum disorders*. New York: Springer.

Mildenberger, K., Sitter, S., Noterdaeme, M., & Amorosa, H. (2001). The use of the ADI-R as a diagnostic tool in the differential diagnosis of children with infantile autism and children with a receptive language disorder. *European Child and Adolescent Psychiatry, 10*, 248–255.

Miller, M.T., & Strömland, K. (1999). Teratogen update: A review, with a focus on ocular findings and new potential uses. *Teratology, 60*, 306–321.

Mirenda, P. (2003). Test review of the Asperger Syndrome Diagnostic Scale. From B.S. Plake, J.C. Impara, & R.A. Spies (Eds.), *The Fifteenth Mental Measurements Yearbook* [Electronic version]. Retrieved December 23, 2003, from the Buros Institute's *Test Reviews Online* web site: http://www.unl.edu/buros

Morgan, S. (1988). Diagnostic assessment of autism: A review of objective scales. *Journal of Psychoeducational Assessment, 6*, 139–151.

Muhle, R., Trentacoste, S.V., & Rapin, I. (2004). The genetics of autism. *Pediatrics, 111*, 472–486.

Mullen, E.M. (1995). *Mullen Scales of Early Learning, AGS Edition*. Circle Pines, MN: American Guidance Service.

Myles, B.S., Bock, S.J., & Simpson, R.L. (2001). *Asperger Syndrome Diagnostic Scale (ASDS)*. Austin, TX: Pro-Ed.

National Institute of Mental Health. (1997, September). *Autism*. [NIH Pub. No. 97–4023]. Bethesda, MD.

National Research Council, Committee on Educational Interventions for Children with Autism. (2001). *Educating Children with Autism*. Washington, DC: National Academy Press.

Neuwirth, S., & Segal, J. (1997). *Autism*. Bethesda, MD: National Institute of Mental Health.

Newschaffer, C.J., Fallin, D., & Lee, N.L. (2002). Heritable and nonheritable risk factors for autism spectrum disorders. *Epidemiologic Reviews, 24*, 137–153.

Nickel, R.E. (1996). Controversial therapies for young children with developmental disabilities. *Infants and Young Children, 8*, 29–40.

Nicolson, R., & Szatmari, P. (2003). Genetic and neurodevelopmental influences in autistic disorder. *Canadian Journal of Psychiatry, 48*, 526–537.

Nordin, V., & Gillberg, C. (1996). Autism spectrum disorders in children with physical or mental disability or both. I: Clinical and epidemiological aspects. *Developmental Medicine and Child Neurology, 38*, 297–213.

Noterdaeme, M., Mildenberger, K., Sitter, S., & Amorosa, H. (2002). Parent information and direct observation in the diagnosis of pervasive and specific developmental disorders. *Autism, 6*, 159–168.

O'Connor, M.E., & Rich, D. (1999). Children with moderately elevated lead levels: Is chelation with DMSA helpful? *Clinical Pediatrics, 38*, 325–331.

O'Neill, R.E., Horner, R.H., Albin, R.W., Sprague, J.R., Storey, K., & Newton, J.S. (1997). *Functional Assessment and Program Development for Problem Behavior: A Practical Handbook* (2nd ed.). Pacific Grove, CA: Brooks/Cole.

Ozonoff, S. (2003, August 7). *Early Identification of Autism.* M.I.N.D. Summer Institute on Neurodevelopmental Disorders, Sacramento, CA.

Ozonoff, S., & Rogers, S. (2003). From Kanner to the millennium. In S. Ozonoff, S.J. Rogers, & R.L. Hendren (Eds.), *Autism Spectrum Disorders: A Research Review for Practitioners* (pp. 3–33). Washington, DC: American Psychiatric Press.

Ozonoff, S., Dawson, G., & McPartland, J. (2002). *A Parent's Guide to Asperger Syndrome and High Functioning Autism: How to Meet the Challenges and Help Your Child Thrive.* New York: Guilford.

Pierce, K., & Schreibman, L. (1997). Multiple peer use of pivotal response training to increase social behaviors of classmates with autism: Results from trained and untrained peers. *Journal of Applied Behavior Analysis, 30*, 157–160.

Powell, J.E., Edwards, A., Edwards, M., Pandit, B.S., Sungum-Paliwal, S.R., & Whitehouse, W. (2000). Changes in incidence of childhood autism and other autistic spectrum disorders from two areas of the West Midlands, UK. *Developmental Medicine and Child Neurology, 42*, 624–628.

Prizant, B.M. (1992). Test review of the Childhood Autism Rating Scale. From J.J. Kramer & J.C. Conoley (Eds.), *The Eleventh Mental Measurements Yearbook* [Electronic version]. Retrieved December 23, 2003, from the Buros Institute's *Test Reviews Online* web site: http://www.unl.edu/buros

Prizant, B., & Wetherby, A. (1998). Understanding the continuum of discrete-trial traditional behavioral to social-pragmatic developmental approaches in communication enhancement for young children with autism/PDD. *Seminars in Speech and Language, 19*, 329–353.

Quintana, H., Birmaher, B., Stedge, D., Lennon, S., Freed, J., Bridge, J., & Greenhill, L. (1995). Use of methylphenidate in the treatment of children with autistic disorders. *Journal of Autism and Developmental Disorders, 25*, 283–294.

Rapin, I., & Katzman, R. (1998). Neurobiology of autism. *Annals of Neurology, 43*, 7–14.

Rau, J.D. (2003, April 1). Is it autism? *Contemporary Pediatrics, 4*. Retrieved December 30, 2004, from http://www.athealth.com/apps/redirect.cfm?linkid=171

Reese, R.M., Richnam, D.M., Zarcone, J., & Zarcone, T. (2003). Individualizing functional assessments for children with autism: The contribution of perseverative behavior and sensory disturbances to disruptive behavior. *Focus on Autism and Other Developmental Disabilities, 18*, 87–92.

Report to the legislature on the principle findings from the Epidemiology of Autism in California. (2002, October 17). *A Comprehensive Pilot Study.* Davis, CA: University of California, Davis, M.I.N.D. Institute.

Research Units on Pediatric Psychopharmacology Autism Network. (2 children with autism and serious behavioral problems. *New England J 347*, 314–321.

Reynolds, C.R., & Kamphaus, R.W. (1998). *BASC: Behavior Assessmen dren.* Circle Pines, MN: American Guidance Services.

Reynolds, C.R., & Richmond, B.O. (1998). *Children's Manifest Anxiety Sca* CA: Western Psychological Services.

Ritvo, E., Freeman, B.J., Pingree, C., Mason-Brothers, A., Jorde, L., McMahon, W.M., Peterson, P.B., Mo, A., & Ritvo, A. (1989). The UCLA– Utah epidemiologic survey of autism: Prevalence. *American Journal of Psy* 194–199.

Ritvo, E.R., Mason-Brothers, A., Freeman, B.J., Pingree, C., Jenson, W.R., W.M., Peterson, P.B., Jorde, L.B., Mo, A., & Ritvo, A. (1990). The UCLA– of Utah epidemiological survey of autism: The etiologic role of rare diseases. *Journal of Psychiatry, 147*, 1612–1614.

Robins, D., Fein, D., Barton, M., & Green, J. (2001). The Modified Checklist for in Toddlers: An initial study investigating the early detection of autism and pe developmental disorders. *Journal of Autism and Developmental Disorders, 31*, 13

Rogan, W.J., Dietrich, K.N., Ware, J.H. Dockery, D.W., Salganik, M., Radcliffe, J., R.L., Ragan, N.B., Chisolm, J.J., Jr., & Rhoads, G.G. (2001). The effect of chel therapy with succimer on neuropsychological development in children exposed to l *New England Journal of Medicine, 344*, 1421–1426.

Rogers, S.J. (1998). Empirically supported comprehensive treatments for young childr with autism. *Journal of Clinical Child Psychology, 27*, 167–178.

Rogers, S.J. (2001). Diagnosis of autism before the age of 3. In L.M. Glidden (Ed.), *Inter national Review of Research in Mental Retardation* (Vol. 23, pp. 1–31). San Diego, CA: Academic Press.

Rogers, S.J., & DiLalla, D. (1991). A comparative study of a developmentally based preschool curriculum on young children with autism and young children with other disorders of behavior and development. *Topics in Early Childhood Special Education, 11*, 29–48.

Rogers, S.J., & Lewis, H. (1989). An effective day treatment model for young children with pervasive developmental disorders. *Journal of the American Academy Child and Adolescent Psychiatry, 28*, 207–214.

Rogers, S.J., Bennetto, L., McEvoy, R., & Pennington, B.F. (1996). Imitation and pantomime in high functioning adolescents with autism spectrum disorders. *Child Development, 67*, 2060–2073.

Rogers, S.J., Hall, T., Osaki, D., Reaven, J., & Herbison, J. (2001). The Denver model: A comprehensive integrated educational approach to young children with autism and their families. In J.S. Handleman & S.L. Harris (Eds.), *Preschool Education Programs for Children with Autism* (2nd ed., pp. 95–134). Austin, TX: Pro-Ed.

Roid, G.H. (2003). *Stanford–Binet Intelligence Scales* (5th ed.). Chicago, IL: Riverside.

Roid, G.H., & Miller, L.J. (1997). *Leiter International Performance Scale—Revised.* Wood Dale, IL: Stoelting.

Rutter, M., Bailey, A., & Lord, C. (2003). *Social Communication Questionnaire.* Los Angeles, CA: Western Psychological Services.

Rutter, M., Le Couteur, A., & Lord, C. (2003). *Autism Diagnostic Interview—Revised: WPS Edition.* Los Angeles, CA: Western Psychological Services.

Sattler, J.M. (1988). *Assessment of Children* (3rd ed.). San Diego, CA: Sattler Publishing.

Sparrow, S.S., Balla, D., & Cicchetti, D. (1984). *Vineland Adaptive Behavior Scales*. Circle Pines, MN: American Guidance Service.

Stahmer, A.C., Ingersoll, B., & Koegel, R.L. (2004). Inclusive programming for toddlers autism spectrum disorders: Outcomes from the Children's Toddler School. *Journal of Positive Behavior Interventions, 6*, 67–82.

Steingard, R.J., Zimnitzky, B., DeMaso, D.R., Bauman, M.L., & Bucci, J.P. (1997). Sertraline treatment of transition-associated anxiety and agitation in children with autistic disorder. *Journal of Child and Adolescent Psychopharmacology, 7*, 9–15.

Strock, M. (2004). *Autism Spectrum Disorders (Pervasive Developmental Disorders)*. [NIH Publication No. NIH-04-5511] Bethesda, MD: National Institute of Mental Health, National Institutes of Health, U.S. Department of Health and Human Services. Retrieved December 19, 2004, from www.nimh.nih.gov/publicat/autism.cfm

Sturmey, P. (2005). Secretin is an ineffective treatment for pervasive developmental disabilities: A review of 15 double-blind randomized controlled trials. *Research in Developmental Disabilities, 26*, 87–97.

Stutsman, R. (1931). Guide for administering the Merrill–Palmer scale of mental tests. In L.M. Terman (Ed.), *Mental Measurement of Preschool Children* (pp. 139–262). New York: Harcourt, Brace and World.

Szatmari, P. (2004). *A proposal to Base the Classification of Autism Spectrum Disorder on Family Genetic Findings*. 2004 Distinguished Lecturer Series, M.I.N.D. Institute, University of California, Davis, Sacramento, CA.

Tharp, B.R. (2003). Contributions of neurology. In S. Ozonoff, S.J. Rogers, & R.L. Hendren (Eds.), *Autism Spectrum Disorders: A Research Review for Practioners* (pp. 111–129). Washington, DC: American Psychiatric Press.

The National Autistic Society. (2004). *Autism and Genetics: A Briefing Paper*. Retrieved December 7, 2004, from http://www.nas.org.uk

Tidmarsh, L., & Volkmar, F.R. (2003). Diagnosis and empidemiology of autism spectrum disorders. *Canadian Journal of Psychiatry, 48*, 517–525.

Travis, L., & Sigman, D. (2000). A developmental approach to autism. In A.J. Sameroff, M. Lewis, & S.M. Miller (Eds.), *Handbook of Developmental Psychopathology* (2nd ed.; pp. 641–655), New York: Kluwer Academic/Plenum Publishers.

U.S. Department of Education (2005, June 10). IDEA 2004: Proposed Changes to the Code of Federal Regulations. Washington, DC. Retrieved July 30, 2005, from http://login.yahoo.com/config/login?.partner=sbc&.done=http%3a//shc.yahoo.com/

U.S. Department of Education, Office of Special Education Programs. (2005). *Annual Report Tables* [Data file]. Available from IDEAdata.org web site, http://www.ideadata.org/AnnualTables.asp

Volkmar, F.R., & Cohen, D.J. (1986). Current concepts: Infantile autism and the pervasive developmental disorders. *Journal of Developmental and Behavioral Pediatrics, 7*, 324–329.

Wakefield, A.J. (2002). Enterocolitis, autism and measles virus. *Molecular Psychiatry, 7*(suppl 2), S44–S46.

Wechsler, D. (1992). *Wechsler Individual Achievement Test*. San Antonio, TX: Psychological Corporation.

Wechsler, D. (1997). *Wechsler Adult Intelligence Scale* (3rd ed.). San Antonio, TX: Psychological Corporation.

Wechsler, D. (1999). *Wechsler Abbreviated Scale of Intelligence*. San Antonio, TX: Psychological Corporation.

Wechsler, D. (2002). *Wechsler Preschool and Primary Scale of Intelligence* (3rd ed.). San Antonio, TX: Psychological Corporation.

Wechsler, D. (2003). *Wechsler Intelligence Scale for Children* (4th ed.). (WISC–IV). San Antonio, TX: Psychological Corporation.

Welsh, J.S. (1992). Test review of the Childhood Autism Rating Scale. From J.J. Kramer & J.C. Conoley (Eds.), *The Eleventh Mental Measurements Yearbook* [Electronic version]. Retrieved December 23, 2003, from the Buros Institute's *Test Reviews Online* web site: http://www.unl.edu/buros

Wheelwright, S. (1995). Questions and answers about the CHAT. London: The National Autistic Society. Retrieved August 2, 2003, from www. nas.org.uk/profess/chat.html

Wing, L. (1991). The relationship between Asperger's syndrome and Kanner's autism. In U. Firth (Ed.), *Autism and Asperger Syndrome* (pp. 93–121). New York: Cambridge University Press.

Woodcock, R.W., McGrew, K.S., & Mather, N. (2001). *Woodcock–Johnson III Tests of Achievement.* Chicago, IL: Riverside Publishing.

Wong, V., Hui, L.S., Lee, W.C., Leung, L.J., Ho, P.P., Lau, W.C., Fung, C.W., & Chung, B. (2004). A modified screening tool for autism (Checklist of Autism in Toddlers [CHAT-23]) for Chinese children. *Pediatrics, 114*, 166–176.

Xu, J., Zwaigenbaum, L., Szatmari, P., & Scherer, S.W. (2004). Molecular cytogenetics of autism. *Current Genomics, 5*, 347–364.

Yale Child Study Center. (n.d.). *Childhood Disintegrative Disorder.* Retrieved December 31, 2004, from http://info.med.yale.edu/chldstdy/autism/cdd.html

Yeargin-Allsopp, M., Rice, C., Karapukar, T., Doernberg, N., Boyle, C., & Murphy, C. (2003). Prevalence of autism in a US metropolitan area. *JAMA, 289*, 49–55.

Young, R., & Brewer, N. (2002). Diagnosis of autistic disorder: Problems and new directions. In L.M. Glidden (Ed.), *International Review of Research in Mental Retardation* (Vol. 25, pp. 107–134). Burlington MA: Academic Press.

Index

A

AA *see* Atypical autism
AAPEP *see* Adolescent and Adult
    Psychoeducational Profile
Abnormal serotonin metabolism, 20
Academic/developmental functioning, 86
Adaptive behavior domains, 85
Additive threshold model of, 14
ADI-R *see* Autism Diagnostic
    Interview—Revised
Adolescent and Adult Psychoeducational Profile,
    87
ADOS *see* Autism Diagnostic Observation
    Schedule
Adult-mediated social interventions, 93
Alpha-adrenergic agonists medications, 95
Alternative and complementary treatments for
    autism, 96
American Psychiatric Association, 3
Antidepressant medication, 95
APA *see* American Psychiatric Association
Appropriate educational curriculum for children
    with autism, 92
A.S.A.S *see* Australian Scale for Asperger's
    Syndrome
ASD *see* autism spectrum disorder
ASDS *see* Asperger Syndrome Diagnostic Scale
Asperger's Disorder, 2, 5–6
Asperger Syndrome Diagnostic Scale, 69
Asperger Syndrome Quotient, 69
ASQ *see* Asperger Syndrome Quotient
Assessment of cognitive function, 82
ASSQ *see* Autism Spectrum Screening
    Questionnaire
Atypical
    autism, 26
    neuroleptics, 94

Audiological assessment in screening for autism,
    39
Autism
    as specific education.eligibility.category, 21
    and special education services, 7
    average age of children for diagnosis, 2
    brain chemistry, 19–20
    brain growth, 16
    brain structure, 10–11
    case finding efforts, 33
    causes of, 10–20
    definition of, 8
    disorder contemporary classification of, 3
    environmental factors in, 14
    genetic and chromosomal abnormalities,
        11–12, 31
    genetics of, 10–14
    index, 69
    mental retardation, 30
    neurological disorders, 31
    organic etiology, 10, 29
    spectrum disorder of, 3
    warning signs of, 33, 35
Autistic Diagnostic Interview—Revised, 70
Autism Diagnostic Observation Schedule, 70, 72
Autistic Disorder symptom onset, 58 59
Autism Spectrum Screening Questionnaire, 45,
    47
Australian Scale for Asperger's Syndrome, 48,
    52
Availability of resources for children with
    autism, 27
Average age of diagnosis of autism, 2

B

Behavior rating scales, 39
Below Average probabilities of autism, 69

Brain's arousal-modulating systems, 19
Brain structures in autism, 10–11

C

CA *see* Childhood autism, 26
CARS *see* Childhood Autism Rating Scale
CAST *see* Childhood Asperger Syndrome Test
Category of Pervasive Developmental Disorders, 3
Causes of autism, 10–20
Changes in autism diagnostic criteria, 26
CHAT *see* CHecklist for Autism in Toddlers
CHecklist for Autism in Toddlers, 39–41
Childhood Asperger Syndrome Test, 48–50
Childhood Autism Rating Scale, 72
Childhood autism, 26
Childhood Disintegrative Disorder, 6
Combination of genetic predisposition, 10
Comprehensive
  examination of language functioning, 85
  preschool intervention programs, 91
  preschool treatment programs, 89
  psycho-educational evaluation of student with autism, 85
Conceptualizations of autism spectrum disorders, 3
Conversational reciprocity of children with Asperger's Disorder, 6
Criteria for Childhood Disintegrative Disorder, 56

D

Data from
  classroom observations, 77
  parents and teachers interviews, 77
  survey conducted in United Kingdom, 2
Data on autism spectrum disorders, 25–26
Developmental screening techniques, 36–37
Diagnostic and Statistical Manual, 3
Diagnostic criteria for
  Autistic Disorder, 55
  Rett's Disorder, 58
Diagnostic evolution
  diagnostic history, 67
  family history, 67
  medical history, 67
Direct Assessment, 71
Distinct pattern of regression, 6
DSM *see* Diagnostic and Statistical Manual
DSMIV-TR
  criteria of, 8, 59
  diagnosis, 54, 56

E

Early identification of Autin, 2
Educational interventions for
  school-age students, 91
  specific target skills, 92
Educational programs
  for school-age children, 91
  planning, 83
Effective behavior intervention programs, 94
Effects of autistic behavior on test validity, 75
Environmental factors in autism
  obstetric suboptimality, 14, 62
  prenatal, 14–15, 62
  postnatal factors, 15, 62
Epistatic model of, 14
Evaluation of student's emotional/behavioral status, 87
Evolution of term autism, 3
Example of child with Autistic Disorder, 4
Explanation of increased rates of autism, 27–28
Expression of Autistic Disorder, 60
Expressive One-Word Picture Vocabulary Test, 85

F

Federal definition of autism, 8
Form of spectrum of autistic disorders, 3
Functional behavioral assessment, 78

G

GABA *see* Gamma-amino butyric acid
Gamma-amino butyric acid
  inhibition of, 20
GARS-2 *see* Gilliam Autism Rating Scale—Second Edition
GARS subtest standard scores, 69
Genetics of autism, 10–14
  candidate gene searches, 12–13
  cytogenetic studies, 12
  genome searches, 12–13
Gilliam Autism Rating Scale—Second Edition, 68

H

Hearing tests for autism screening, 39
Heller's syndrome, 6
Hypotheses of impaired neurotransmission in autism, 20

I

ICD *see* International Classification of Diseases
Incidence of autism classification, 22

IDEA *see* Individuals with Disabilities
    Education Act
IDEA
    as controlling authority, 8
    data of, 23
    requirement of, 8
    special education eligibility classification, 27
IDEIA *see* Individuals with Disabilities
    Education Improvement Act
Identification of autism genes, 12–13
IEP *see* Individual Educational Planning
Indirect assessment, 68
Individual Educational Planning, 8
Individuals with Disabilities Education Act, 1
Individuals with Disabilities Education
    Improvement Act, 7
Infantile autism term of, 3, 26
Intelligence test performance, 83
International Classification of Diseases, 26
IQ test results, 83

L

Lead screening for autism screening, 38

M

Male to female ratio for disorders, 60–61
M-CHAT *see* Modified Checklist of Autism in
    Toddlers
Minimal professional requirements
    in diagnosis of autism spectrum disorder,
    54–55
Minimization of distraction, 76
Model intervention programs, 92
Modified Checklist of Autism in Toddlers,
    41–43
Modulation of immune function for treatment,
    97

N

Neurobiology, 15–20
    brain size of, 15–18
    brain structure of, 18–19
    brain chemistry of, 19–20
Neuroleptics, 94
Novel testing room environment, 75
Number of students with autism, 7

O

Observation of student with autism in typical
    environments, 78
Obstetric suboptimality, 14
Organic etiology of autin, 10, 29
Overall global intelligence test score, 84

P

Pattern of head growth deceleration, 7
Peer-mediated interventions, 93
PEP-3 *see* Psychoeducational Profile—Third
    Edition
PDD *see* Pervasive Developmental Disorders
Peabody Picture Vocabulary Test, 85
PECS *see* Picture Exchange Communication
    System
Percentage of children with Autistic Disorder, 2
Pervasive Developmental Disorder, 3–4
Pervasive Developmental Disorder Not
    Otherwise Specified, 3, 6
Pervasive Developmental Disorders Screening
    Test-II, 70
PDD-NOS *see* Pervasive Developmental
    Disorder Not Otherwise Specified
PDD-NOS diagnostic classification of, 6
PDDST-II *see* Pervasive Developmental
    Disorders Screening Test-II
Picture Exchange Communication System, 92
Pivotal response training, 90
Polymorphism of autism genes, 13
Pragmatic communication among verbal
    children with autism, 93
Prevalence of autism, 2, 27–28
Primary symptoms of Autistic Disorder, 4
Prenatal factors of, 14–15, 62
    drug exposure of, 14
    maternal infection, 14
Preparation of students for testing experiments,
    75
Progressive developmental disorder, 7
PRT *see* Pivotal response training
Psychoeducational
    assessments of, 74–75, 78
    evaluation of, 62
    testing of, 78
Psychoeducational Profile—Third Edition, 86
Psychopharmacologic interventions, 94
Psychometric data, 42
Psychostimulant medication, 95
Public awareness of autism, 27

R

Rate of autism in general population, 23
Research Units of Pediatric
    Psychopharmacology's
    Autism Network, 94–95
Red flags of autism
    behavioral concerns, 37
    communication concerns, 36–37
    social concerns, 36–37

Relationship between thimerosal-containing
      vaccines and autism, 15
Removal of toxins, 97
Rett's Disorder among females, 7
Review of behavioral observation, 77–78
Risk factors signals for symptoms of autism,
      34–35
Risks of alternative therapies, 96
Role of genetic factors in autism, 10

S
School-based developmental screenings of, 36
School professionals
   in identification process of, 2
   knowledge of autism, 2
SCQ *see* Social Communication Questionnaire
Screening tools for
   infants, 39
   preschoolers, 39
   schoolage children, 45
Sign language in teaching communication, 93
Social Communication Questionnaire, 48, 50
Social interaction difficulties with autism, 58–59
Specific conditions associated with autism
   social class, 29
   race, 29
Specific psycho educational assessment practice,
      77
Standardized administration for test, 77
Strongest objective scale for diagnosis of autism,
      72

Student's
   relative pattern of strengths, 77
   relative pattern of weakness, 77
   test performance, 77
Students with autism served under IDEA, 21–25
Subjective nature of indirect assessment, 68
Symptom of
   delayed communication
   impaired communication, 4
   warning signs of autism

T
TEACCH program, 90–91
Testing
   accommodations, 75
   modifications, 75
   session in student's schedule, 75
Treatment of autism spectrum disorder, 88–97
Treatments purported to alter neurotransmitter
      release, 96

U
Use of
   preestablished physical structure, 76
   powerful external rewards, 76
   work systems, 76

W
Warning signs of autism, 33, 35
Wechsler Individual Achievement Test, 87
Woodcock–Johnson Tests of Achievement, 87